The Prestige S

Sentinel

Buses and Coaches

John Howie & Neville Mercer

with additional material by John Banks

© 2005 J Howie & N Mercer
ISBN 1 898432 50 3

All rights reserved. Except for normal review purposes no part of this book may be reproduced or utilised in any form or by any means, electrical or mechanical, including photocopying, recording or by an information storage and retrieval system, without the prior written consent of Venture Publications Ltd, Glossop, Derbyshire.

Front cover: The most familiar Sentinels were those in the Ribble fleet. The Preston operator had 14 of the STC6 model, of which No. **289** (**DRN 346**) was originally allocated to Carlisle but worked from Penrith between 1956 and 1962. Withdrawn in 1963, after spending a final year with Ribble allocated to Ulverston, it served a contractor in Nottinghamshire before being scrapped in 1968. It is pictured in the depot yard at Penrith with blinds set for the route to Brothers Water. *(G W Dickson Collection)*

Back cover: A Park Royal-bodied Sentinel SLC6/42 that was exhibited at the Commercial Motor Show in 1950, before export to Viacao Nacional, Rio de Janeiro, Brazil. Five more similar vehicles were originally ordered (and allocated body numbers by Park Royal) but never delivered. Nothing is known of its Brazilian registration and history. *(Senior Transport Archive)*

Title page: The Boyer, of Rothley, Sentinels maintained a high profile, particularly when two of them passed into the Midland Red fleet. **GUT 543** was at St Margarets, Leicester, in March 1952, some seven years before becoming Midland Red No. 4847. *(G H F Atkins/© & Courtesy John Banks Collection)*

Opposite page: Ribble Motor Services took delivery of the third prototype of Sentinel's 40-seat service bus in May 1949 as fleet number **2722** (**CRN 211**). It was immediately placed into service on route 109 between Preston and Chorley, which chanced to pass the gates of Leyland Motors Ltd; perhaps Ribble was sending Leyland a message? *(Senior Transport Archive)*

Below: Chassis SLC 6/42/36 was originally intended for Brazil, then Uruguay, but was delivered to Portugal, entering the fleet of Viacao da Beira, Pampilhosa da Serra, as **GC-18-68** in September 1952. The builder of the original body (seen here) is not recorded. It later received new UTIC bodywork and a Leyland engine before joining the Rodoviaria Nacional fleet.

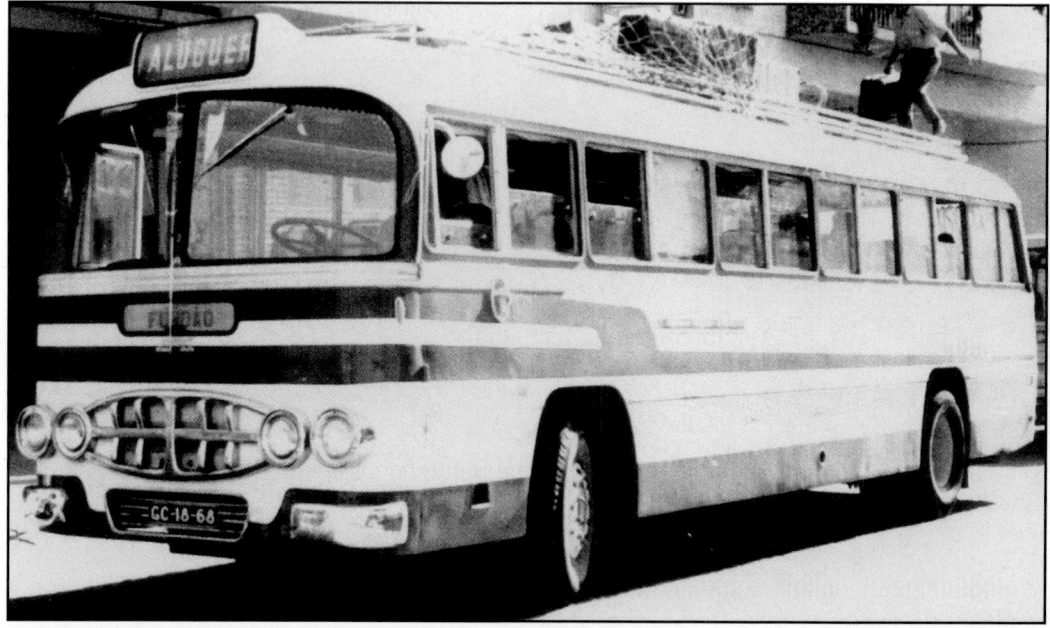

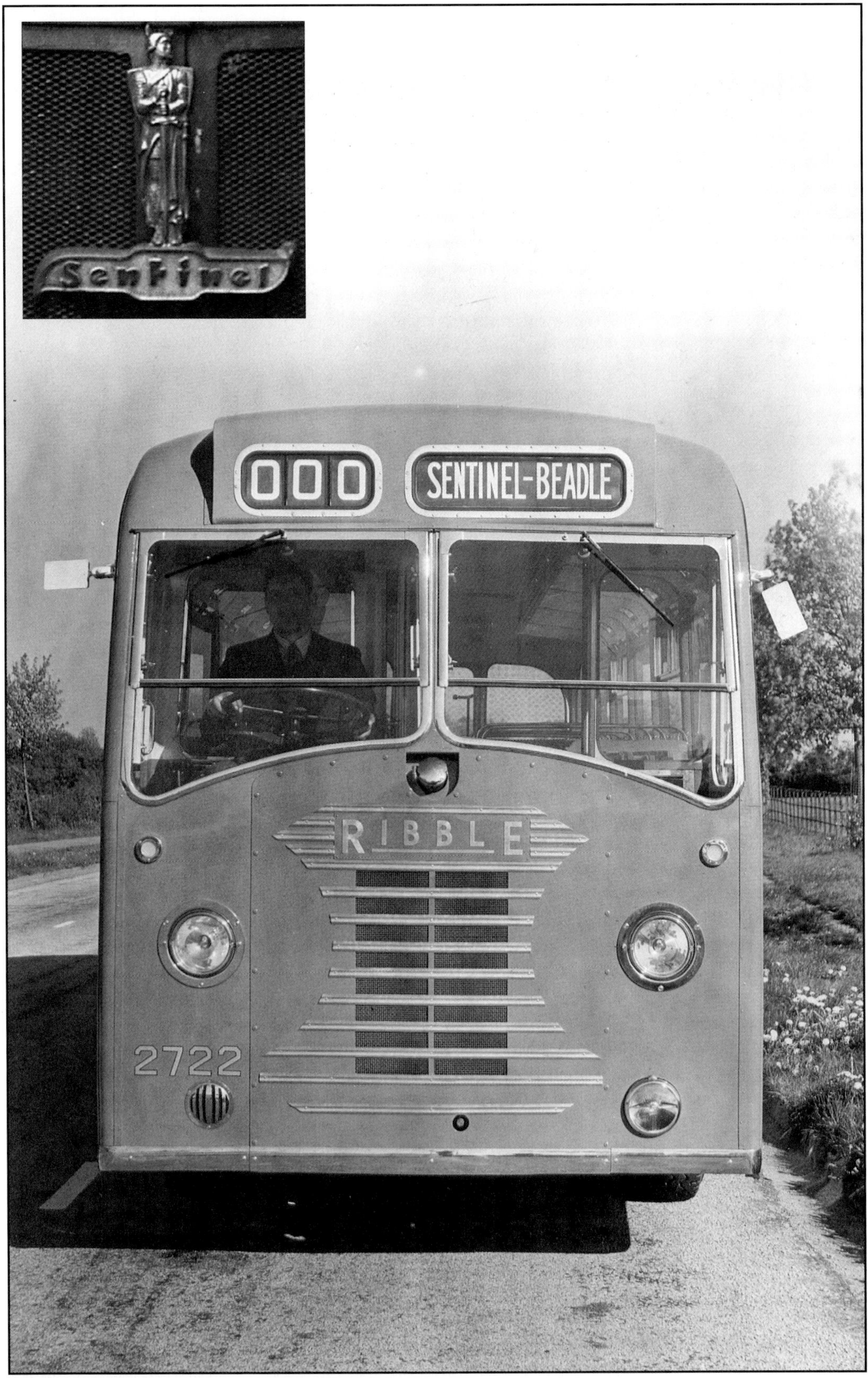
Sentinel
000
SENTINEL-BEADLE
RIBBLE
2722

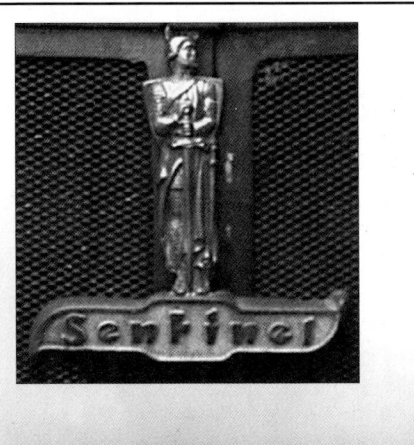

TABLE OF CONTENTS

1.	Introduction and Acknowledgements	Page 4
2.	A brief history of Sentinel	8
3.	Sentinel buses and coaches 1948-1956	12
4.	Technical data	28
5.	What the papers said	32
6.	Sentinels in service	38
7.	Individual vehicle histories	44
8.	Stage-carriage operators	78
9.	Non-PSV users	118
10.	Derelicts and dealers	124
11.	Sentinels in preservation	129
12.	Registration number index	137
13.	A Sentinel Miscellany	138

INTRODUCTION AND ACKNOWLEDGEMENTS

Sentinels were rare. Not as rare as Jensen JLPs, Rowe Hillmasters, or Rutland Clippers, but nonetheless rare enough, and their rarity was undoubtedly a major part of their appeal to the bus enthusiast. And appeal they undoubtedly did. A recurring theme of the letters received during the research for this book has been the element of 'pilgrimage' on the part of our correspondents, who have collectively travelled many thousands of miles (often to obscure communities) in their quest for the marque.

Rarity alone cannot account for such devotion and it seems unlikely that similar journeys have been undertaken in search of (equally scarce) Atkinson Alphas or underfloor-engined Guy Arabs. Sentinels were different. They had charisma. Back in 1948 they had been the James Dean of the British bus industry, a young iconoclastic upstart that dared to be first with a new concept and then carried it to market a clear two years ahead of its Establishment competitors at AEC and Leyland. Then came the roller-coaster ride with the peak of the Ribble order being followed by the trough of the engine problems, the despair of lost opportunity by the hope of a return in triumph ... and then the inevitable climax as the track ran out beneath their wheels.

For all their modern promise, born in an age when the half-cab single-decker still reigned supreme, the Sentinels had some curiously old-fashioned aspects to them - not least the indirect injection engines. These purred delightfully, were quieter and smoother than any diesel engine before or since, and had only two bad points - poor reliability and massive fuel consumption. The reliability problem was solved by an expensive change to a direct injection system which reduced available power by more than 12%. For the 4-cylinder machines this could be a problem, but the 6-cylinder machines were still powerful beasts as anyone who has travelled from Penrith to Windermere on one will bear witness.

Mention of the Lake District reveals the third reason for the Sentinels' enduring popularity. They not only had rarity and

Above: Ribble was by far the most important operator of Sentinel PSVs, using a total of 20 on routes around Carlisle and in the Lake District. This shot shows STC6/44 **DRN 343** on layover at Coniston after operating a journey on service 500 from its home base at Ulverston. The Sentinels' performance on steep gradients made them popular with Ribble's local drivers.

Below: A brace of SLC4/35 coaches at the premises of Benyon of Atherton (the yard was actually in neighbouring Tyldesley) in the summer of 1951. **NTB 955** on the left was first licensed to Benyon and **NLG 176** on the right was a former demonstrator first registered to the North Cheshire Motors dealership.

charisma, they had location! Ribble's fleet operated amid spectacular scenery and other examples could be found in the resort towns of the Ayrshire coast, in the tourist villages of North Wales and Pembrokeshire, by Cornish coves, and facing a fierce wind at Skegness. Even in resorts such as Blackpool (with no local Sentinel population) a holidaymaking enthusiast might catch sight of STC6/44s from Ribble (on a Carlisle duplicate) and Boyer of Rothley (its passengers numb from the waist down after four hours aboard), not to mention an occasional SLC6/30 coach from any one of a half-dozen Lancashire or Yorkshire firms.

A holiday romance turned into a lifetime's attraction for many a bus enthusiast, and chance encounters by the seaside could lead to irrational expeditions into the depths of Shropshire where Sentinels lived in a land beyond time called Telford New Town. Their custodians, the Browns of Donnington Wood, could justly lay claim to enhancing the local economy, not only by buying locally produced buses but by luring hundreds of bus enthusiasts into the area to take photographs of them. Admittedly there were other exotic PSVs in the Telford / Wellington / Shrewsbury area, but most of these could be better sampled in Cornwall and Devonshire. Enthusiasts went to Telford to see the Sentinel SLC4/35s, in daily use well into the 1970s and several of them were ultimately preserved as their reward for long service.

Inevitably the sad day came when there were no longer any Sentinels in service. And equally inevitably there will soon enough be a day when nobody left alive can remember the sight of one in service. As we approach the fiftieth anniversary of the company's demise a tribute seems appropriate and we hope that this book can serve as a memorial to Sentinel's buses and coaches, to those who designed them and built them, to those who bought and operated them, to those who rode in them, and to all of those who photographed them, recorded their history, and helped to make this publication a possibility.

The authors would like to thank all of those who have contributed to this project, including Ian Bailey, Peter Bowers, Arthur Brazenose (Coordinator of the Sentinel Research Group), Geoff Bruce, Colin L Caddy, Neal Cahill, Bob Cornish, Wilf Dodds, the late Jack Edwards (formerly of Sentinel), Thomas Fowler, Nick Georgano, Cyril Golding, Richard Gray, Grahame Hawkyard (formerly of Whitson), John Hinchliffe, Peter Howie (for assistance with photographic processing), Martin Ingle, Dave Jessop, Philip Kirk, Christopher Lewis, Helena J Mercer (for her invaluable IT help), G R Mills, Paul Moore, Martin Perry, John Rudkin, Chris Taylor, Dr Michael A Taylor, Tony Thomas (of the Sentinel Drivers Club), T G Turner, Andrew Webster, and D L Wheatley.

The photographs included in this book have been kindly provided from the collections of the following individuals and organisations whose assistance has been incalculably valuable: John Banks, A D Broughall, Colin Caddy, C Carter, Bob Cornish, Alan B Cross, Kevin Delaine-Smith, John C Gilham, Nick Georgano, W J Haynes, John Hinchliffe, D A Jones, S E Letts, Christopher Lewis, R F Mack, C D Maun, G R Mills, Paul Moore, P Noonan, H Peers, PM Photography, P S A Redmond, the Ribble Enthusiasts Club, John Senior, M D Shaw, Dr M A Taylor, J C Walker, D L Wheatley, R L Wilson and F W York. We were not able to trace the original photographers for several other illustrations, taken from the authors' collections or that of the Sentinel Research Group, and we would like to thank them for their anonymous efforts which have helped us to make this book more comprehensive.

In addition to these sources we have made extensive use of the publications of both The Omnibus Society and The PSV Circle and of news and feature items in Passenger Transport, Buses Illustrated, Buses, Classic Bus, Bus & Coach Preservation and Buses Worldwide, and thank all concerned for their endeavours. We would also like to express our gratitude to the many bus and coach operators who have taken the time to respond to our letters over the years when they might have been more sensibly employed making money! Theirs is the hardest task of them all.

November 2004
John Howie, Horley, Surrey
Neville Mercer, Bolton

Above: An official factory view showing unidentified STC4/40s in the final assembly shed at Whitchurch Road during 1950. The bodywork was assembled from Beadle-designed parts manufactured by Sentinel's parent company, Metal Industries.

Below: Most sources agree that this double-deck design was never actually built, but it does show that the company was considering the possibility of bus manufacture as early as 1905, the date of the catalogue from which this illustration is taken.

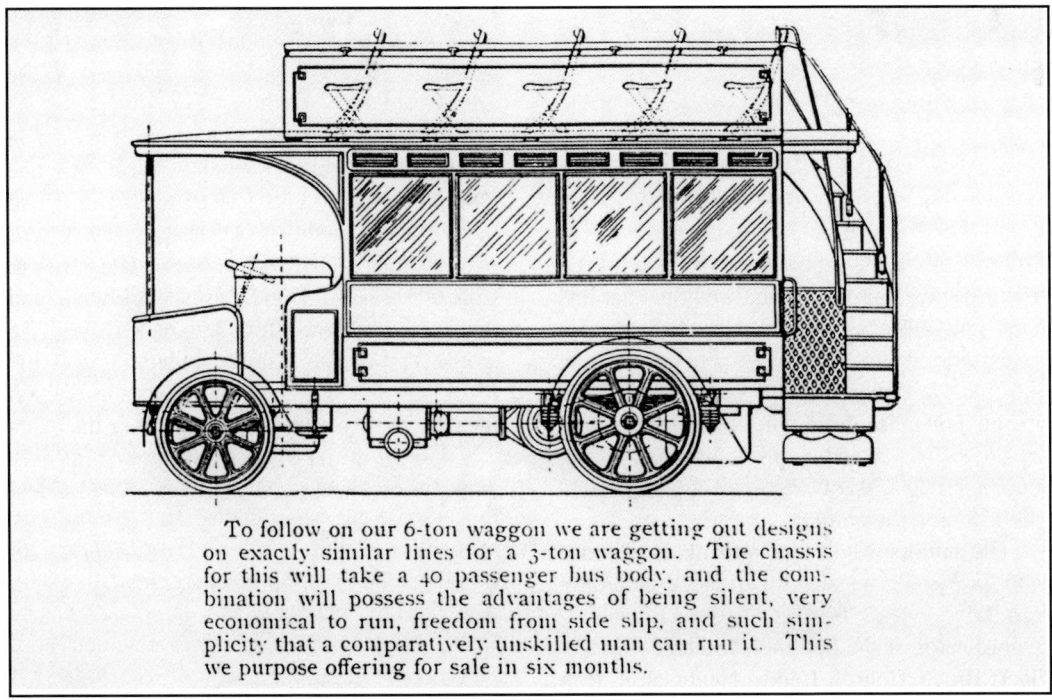

To follow on our 6-ton waggon we are getting out designs on exactly similar lines for a 3-ton waggon. The chassis for this will take a 40 passenger bus body, and the combination will possess the advantages of being silent, very economical to run, freedom from side slip, and such simplicity that a comparatively unskilled man can run it. This we purpose offering for sale in six months.

A BRIEF HISTORY OF SENTINEL

In less than a hundred years the steam engine changed the world. At first, the technology was crude and restricted to static installations designed to run textile machinery or to pump water from mine workings. Within a quarter of a century the engines available had improved in efficiency to the point where a relatively small unit could pull a considerable load of many tons. The railway age had begun. Another quarter of a century and steam engines were poised to shatter the dominion of windpower on the high seas. The technology continued to improve and after thousands of years of supremacy the sailing ship became a curiousity within a single lifetime. By 1870 maritime steam engines had become small enough - and cheap enough - to install in relatively modest vessels, among them the swarming ferryboats of the Clyde estuary and Inner Hebrides. A host of new companies were founded to build and power these vessels, known colloquially as 'puffers', and although most were doomed to an early failure a few of the stronger concerns prospered and diversified.

One of the survivors was a partnership founded in Glasgow in 1875 by Messrs. Stephen Alley and John Alexander MacLellan, trading as the 'Sentinel Engineering Works'. Business was brisk and larger premises were acquired in 1880. Stephen Alley died in 1898 and his share of the partnership passed to his son, Stephen Evans Alley, until a formal company was registered in 1903 under the name Alley and MacLellan Limited. This entity continued to use the Sentinel name and applied it to a new range of steam waggons known as 'Standard Sentinels' which rapidly acquired a first-rate reputation for ruggedness and reliability. Sentinel had come ashore. By 1905 it had become one of the market-leaders in steam waggons and had also tentatively offered a double-decker steam bus in their Standard Sentinel range. Sadly it seems that there were no takers and it remained no more than a blueprint.

The Company's move into road vehicles proved timely as Britain's highways were finally becoming navigable for long-distance haulage, and although steam waggons were slow (in comparison with railways), they offered flexibility and the convenience of door-to-door delivery. Many of the Company's new customers were based in England and, in 1915, a second factory was established in Shrewsbury to meet demand south of the border. The new works, as the inland location suggested, concentrated on road and rail vehicles. Three years later, in May 1918, this became a separate subsidiary, Sentinel Waggon Works Limited, and when the parent company was sold to William Beardmore (a much larger Glasgow engineering group) four months later, the Shrewsbury operation was not included, being sold back to Stephen Evans Alley in exchange for his shares in Alley and MacLellan Limited.

In 1919 Sentinel came close to making a bus again, although it might take a generous definition of such a vehicle for the steam waggon in question to qualify. Registration number AW 3918 was an 'off the peg' Standard Sentinel fitted with longitudinal wooden bench seats and towed a similarly outfitted trailer. It ran in service with Newcastle Corporation, acting as a feeder to trams on a route from Burradon to Lane Ends. This service operated from Monday to Friday and at weekends the benches were removed and the vehicle used to transport horse manure from the Corporation's stables to local farmers. Hardly the most fragrant of public service vehicles, but it served its purpose.

An improved version of the steam waggon, known as the Super Sentinel, sold well during the 1920s and several were equipped with genuine bus bodywork. The prototype of the bus variant, NT 4950, (fitted with a Hora B32R body), was widely demonstrated to British operators but found no customers and after a year or so was relegated to duties as a Sentinel staff-bus during 1925. Overseas sales were hardly more encouraging with single examples going to Czechoslovakia, South Africa and India. In 1927 the bus variant was quietly dropped from the range.

Meanwhile, steam waggons were selling well, the Company's coffers were bulging and the decision was made to expand by acquisition. The target was Henry Garner, of Birmingham, a rival manufacturer of steam waggons; the purchase was completed in late 1926. The Garner works was retained until 1934 when all production was concentrated at

Above: The Super Sentinel was highly successful as a goods chassis, notably less so as a bus. This is **NT 4950**, the company-owned demonstrator, which steamed its way around Britain in search of orders but found not one. Several similar vehicles were sent to Sentinel's overseas dealerships but were met with similar indifference.

Below: A nearside view of **NT 4950** clearly showing the high floor level made necessary by its underfloor power-unit. At around this time Leyland and Maudslay were introducing ranges of vehicles which emphasised their lower frames, making the Super Sentinel look very dated.

Shrewsbury although the Garner name continued with its own separate network of dealers.

Just as the future seemed assured, the 1930 Road Traffic Act delivered a major blow to the company's prospects by taxing Heavy Goods Vehicles according to their unladen weight. By its very nature, a steam waggon was a heavy beast, allowing vehicles propelled by internal combustion engines a substantial economic advantage. Things were made worse by the development, in the early 1930s, of reliable and fuel-efficient diesel engines. As one customer after another opted for diesel power Sentinel's production rate fell from hundreds per year to dozens. In Shrewsbury the sky was falling.

In June 1935 the company's financial problems reached crisis point and a receiver was appointed to protect the interests of its creditors. Garner was sold to a group of American investors to help pay off the company's debts and in November 1936 a slimmed-down business emerged from receivership as Sentinel Waggon Works (1936) Limited. The lesson had been learned and all available resources were thrown into a rapid exodus from the world of steam-powered road vehicles. The Company continued to produce its range of steam locomotives for railway use, a valuable source of income which had helped it to survive receivership while many other manufacturers of steam waggons had plummeted into bankruptcy.

The late 1930s saw the production of diesel-powered lorry prototypes; in October 1937 Sentinel showed interest in another means of propulsion when it acquired the rights to producer-gas technology from High Speed Gas (Great Britain) Limited. High Speed Gas had previously been allied with Gilford until that chassis-maker's demise, and to Stephen Evans Alley - desperate for non-steam alternatives - the chance to acquire some new technology 'on the cheap' must have seemed like a gift from above. The prototype of the Sentinel-HSG bus (actually a Gilford 176 chassis fitted with a Cowieson 32-seat rear-entrance service-bus body) had a Hercules engine adapted for HSG fuel and was demonstrated to several operators including Merthyr Tydfil Corporation and South Wales Transport. It attracted no orders and was later converted to run on petrol before ending up with the Shropshire independent Cooper, of Oakengates.

The HSG purchase did bring one unexpected bonus. During the Second World War severe oil shortages led to many buses and delivery vehicles being temporarily converted to run on gas. Each conversion incorporated components covered by HSG patents and resulted in royalty payments to Sentinel. This, and the continuing demand for railway locomotives (mostly small shunting engines bought by owners of large industrial sites), kept the balance sheets in equilibrium if never quite in measurable profit. As a sole proprietor, with limited financial resources, Stephen Evans Alley could do little to rouse the company from its flat-lining slumbers and in 1941 he sold it to the Metal Industries group, a major industrial conglomerate which had been anxious to expand into vehicle manufacturing. They renamed the company Sentinel (Shrewsbury) Limited.

The end of the war brought a return of the peacetime problems. Steam waggons were effectively finished (although Sentinel continued to produce them in small numbers until 1950), but the cost of a wholesale transition to diesel production seemed beyond the Company's means, even with the benefit of a cash infusion from its new owners. As a cost-cutting measure Sentinel bought a licence to produce a Ricardo-designed indirect injection diesel engine for use in its postwar range of vehicles. With benefit of hindsight we can see that this was a false economy, which led inexorably to the demise of the company.

The problems with the engines became legendary. First of all there was a great reluctance by many customers to accept an indirect injection diesel which was considered to be 'first generation' technology and quite antiquated by postwar standards. On the positive side the engine ran smoothly and quietly and was possessed of more than adequate power. On the negative side it used much more fuel than a comparable direct injection unit and possessed a complexity of parts which could (and frequently did) conspire to malfunction. The engine's tendency to overheat or even catch fire was another less than endearing characteristic. Secondly, Sentinel was a novice in the world of diesel

Above: The chassis of the Sentinel-HSG prototype was essentially a Gilford 176 modified to suit the power-plant. This company shot shows it at Whitchurch Road about to depart on the long journey to bodybuilder Cowieson in Scotland.

Below: The Sentinel-HSG again, after being fitted with a rear-entrance bus body by Cowieson and registration as **AUX 296** by Sentinel. In this 1939 shot the vehicle is seen at the Paddington (London) premises of Charles Rickards Tours. It remains uncertain whether it was on demonstration to them or merely parked overnight while in the capital for other purposes.

engines. The underfloor engine mountings of the DV4 goods range and the related bus models had been poorly designed and tended to fail in the most dramatic fashion imaginable. Sentinel gained an unwelcome place in HGV folklore as the manufacturer whose engines fell out of their vehicles, a reputation that the company's sales force found hard to overcome long after the problems with the engine mountings had been successfully resolved.

Technical problems aside, Sentinel had other difficulties. Their products were competing with those of larger manufacturers with well-established dealer networks and years of experience in producing diesel-powered vehicles. Their hapless salesmen had an unconvincing proposition to make to potential customers, which involved taking a chance on the products of a relative newcomer using an old-fashioned engine of questionable reliability.

Given all of these factors, the sales representatives must have performed admirably to amass the sales that they did - around 1,200 diesel lorries and 135 diesel buses between 1947 and 1956 - but, sadly, this was less than half the break-even factor and the Board of Metal Industries was unimpressed. Even though most of the early problems had been successfully addressed, with a direct injection variant of the Ricardo engine available from 1952 and various other drive-line improvements, the reputation for unreliability had stuck. Worse yet, the market for steam locomotives had begun to decline as the diesel engine captured another market for the petroleum suppliers. Sentinel could no longer rely on profits from the shunting engines to save its corporate neck.

In early 1955 Sentinel's management was told to accept no new orders for diesel-powered road vehicles. Existing orders were completed and limited production of railway locomotives continued while the parent company sought a buyer for the Shrewsbury works. A year and a half later Metal Industries sold the factory to Rolls-Royce and it was quickly transformed into their Sentinel Division, specialising in the production of machine tools and engine parts. The age of the Sentinel had come to an end, its ambitions stymied by a lack of investment and of affordable technology rather than by any lack of enthusiasm, style, genius, or imagination.

SENTINEL BUSES AND COACHES 1948-1956

Metal Industries' decision to buy Sentinel in 1941 offered new opportunities to both parent company and subsidiary. For the MI Group Sentinel provided cheap admission into the ranks of vehicle manufacturing whilst securing a 'captive' market for the metal panelling produced by several of its regional divisions. From Sentinel's viewpoint Metal Industries offered the financial backing to make the Company's dream of a modern diesel-powered range a reality. For a while, with half the workforce away in uniform and priority inevitably given to war-related activities, the diesel project progressed slowly, but designs were finalised and a power-plant selected for licence-production at Shrewsbury.

This was the Ricardo four-cylinder engine with indirect fuel injection which later became known as the 4SRH (4-cylinder Sentinel-Ricardo Horizontal). As the final word suggests, it was to be fitted in an underfloor position on all of the new models, following in the tradition of the Super Sentinel steam-waggon but breaking new ground for diesel vehicles.

First of the new range to emerge was the DV4 diesel lorry (Diesel Vehicle 4-cylinder) which went on general sale in early 1947 and attracted many customers, including several diehard steam-waggon operators who chose the start of the postwar era as their conversion point. In the subsequent twelve months, the DV4 broke the company's own internal sales targets, which had been thought of as too optimistic by some, and was available with three different wheelbases. The longest of these, the 14ft 9ins version, was selected as the basis of the new bus model, the SB4/40 (Sentinel Beadle 4-cylinder/40 seats).

John C Beadle, of Dartford, Kent, had joined the project at the behest of Metal Industries, which provided much of the panelling used in Beadle's existing range of bus and coach bodywork. The Kent bodybuilder's products sold well in the south-east of England, but outside of that area were little seen except

Above: This impressive Super Sentinel bus was exported to Skoda of Czechoslovakia (then the company's distributor in Central Europe) for use as a demonstrator. It is believed that the body was built locally after export. The vehicle was as unsuccessful as its British equivalent and ended its days as a staff bus for Skoda. Note the use of Roman numerals as a component of the registration - a peculiarly Czechoslovakian practice of the inter-war years.

Below: The second SB4/40 prototype received Western National livery as **HOD 57** and duly entered service on the Sidmouth to Taunton route after a brief moment of fame at the 1948 Commercial Motor Show. The location of this company shot is unknown.

in the form of hybrid vehicles that used prewar or war-surplus running units. These vehicles were very much a sympton of the early postwar conditions of austerity and Beadle was anxious to secure a position in the market for underfloor-engined vehicles, which it correctly saw as the future of the single-decker. It must have seemed like another ideal alliance and offered Metal Industries a customer which, while not exactly captive, could find many reasons for loyalty to their products.

The initial prototype of the SB4/40 bus was completed by Beadle in March 1948. It was immediately taken to Shrewsbury for intensive testing before making its public debut in October at the Commercial Motor Show. It appeared at Earls Court in Western National livery and became that company's fleet number 2006 (HOD 57). Sentinel's reputation for unpredictable allocation of construction numbers had its origins at this point, as the first vehicle completed was chassis number SB4/40/2. Things would become more erratic as time went by.

Meanwhile, chassis number SB4/40/1 had materialised in June 1948 as EUJ 792. After six months as a demonstrator it was sold, at an 'attractive' price, to local operator Salopia Saloon Coaches, who used it on their main-line service from Whitchurch to Wem and Shrewsbury. By agreement with Salopia it continued to act as a test vehicle for various improvements to the design and was maintained by Sentinel-employed engineers for the first year after sale.

Sentinel was an undoubted star of the 1948 Show and while HOD 57 impressed those inside Earls Court, EUJ 792 gave demonstration rides to journalists and potential customers alike. Passenger Transport magazine commented favourably on its low unladen weight (5 tons 8 cwts), high seating capacity, and all-metal construction 'with the exception of the wood flooring'. They were also 'very impressed by the liveliness of the engine, its silence, and its private-car performance'. Curiously, the same article in the magazine refers to the vehicle as being 'one of a fleet ordered by the Western National Omnibus Company'. This was completely untrue - in fact WNOC had agreed to accept the vehicle as part of an existing order for Bedford-Beadle integral buses, basically as a spare to cover for unserviceability among the Bedford-based units; a fleet of Western National Sentinels was never a prospect.

Journalists were not the only people to be impressed. Visitors to the Sentinel stand included a delegation from Ribble Motor Services and they really were shopping for a fleet of underfloor-engined buses. It is tempting to imagine the looks on the faces of the Sentinel representatives when the delegation from Ribble introduced themselves. Ribble at that time was one of the largest and most influential bus companies in the British Isles, operating across a huge territory which stretched from the Scottish border to Liverpool and Manchester. Its express services ranged from Glasgow and Edinburgh to London and Cheltenham while its touring coaches were to be found from John o' Groats to Lands End (both were in Ribble tour itineraries). The Preston-based operator was normally a customer of its local chassis-builder, Leyland Motors, but was smitten with the idea of underfloor-engined single-deckers and felt that Leyland were being rather slow in providing such a design. The timing was perfect. Only the particulars needed to be agreed, and Sentinel were inclined to give Ribble whatever they wanted, within reason.

The third prototype of the 40-seat bus was immediately reallocated to Ribble and after much overtime it was completed in January 1949 as fleet number 2722 (CRN 211). It differed from the previous two SB4/40s in many detailed ways, the most obvious of which was a Beadle-style concealed radiator in contrast to the exposed DV4 units previously used. After exhaustive static and mobile testing it was delivered to Preston in May and immediately placed into service on route 109 between Preston and Chorley.

Right: *The very first Sentinel diesel bus, SB4/40* **EUJ 792***, proudly displayed in an advertisement wearing Salopia livery and en route for Market Drayton. The vehicle did appear on this service but was more usually found on the Whitchurch-Wem-Shrewsbury route. The first two prototypes had DV4 lorry front panels and radiator grilles even though their bodywork was assembled by Beadle.*

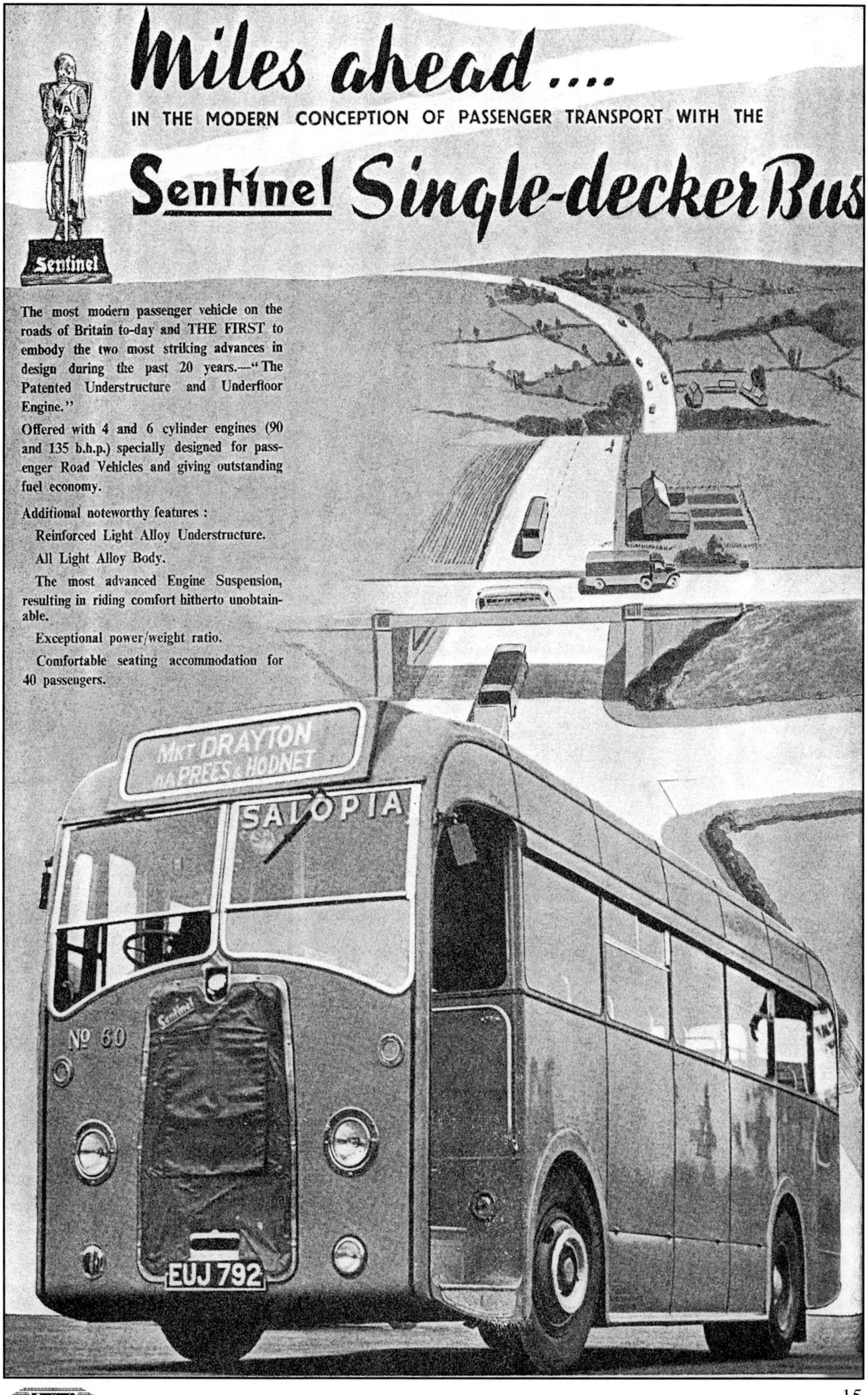

Miles ahead....
IN THE MODERN CONCEPTION OF PASSENGER TRANSPORT WITH THE
Sentinel Single-decker Bus

The most modern passenger vehicle on the roads of Britain to-day and THE FIRST to embody the two most striking advances in design during the past 20 years.—"The Patented Understructure and Underfloor Engine."

Offered with 4 and 6 cylinder engines (90 and 135 b.h.p.) specially designed for passenger Road Vehicles and giving outstanding fuel economy.

Additional noteworthy features :
 Reinforced Light Alloy Understructure.
 All Light Alloy Body.
 The most advanced Engine Suspension, resulting in riding comfort hitherto unobtainable.
 Exceptional power/weight ratio.
 Comfortable seating accommodation for 40 passengers.

The 109 passed through Leyland (possibly by more than a happy coincidence) providing a regular reminder that Ribble had gone elsewhere for its latest bus. CRN 211 seems to have behaved well during evaluation, as Ribble subsequently placed an order for 19 more vehicles, five of them virtually identical to the prototype, the remaining fourteen of a new 30ft variant with 44 seats and a six-cylinder version of the Ricardo engine. The impact of this order could not be overestimated. With the exception of an occasional demonstrator or vehicles bought during wartime, all of Ribble's new vehicles for more than thirty years had been Leylands. In every conceivable sense of the phrase, Sentinel's buses had arrived.

Great expectations

In late 1949 it was decided to change the designation of the bus model from SB4/40 to STC4/40, possibly to reflect the fact that all future bus bodywork would be assembled at Shrewsbury rather than at Beadle's works in Kent. The exact meaning of this new designation remains ambiguous, with a former member of the Company's engineering staff asserting that it signified 'Sentinel Transit Coach' (following American practice of the time), while contemporary sales brochures and advertisements make repeated use of the phrase 'Sentinel Town and Country'. At the same time the 44-seat bus development became the STC6/44, indicating its use of a six-cylinder engine (the 6SRH), and the new coach model became the SLC4/35 (Sentinel Luxury Coach, 4-cylinder/35 seats). There was also an SLC6/42 model designed for export which featured left-hand drive and was suitable for bodywork up to 33ft in length.

It should be noted at this point that the semi-integral bodywork fitted to both STC4/40 and STC6/44 vehicles was (as a rule) assembled at Shrewsbury from components supplied by Welsh Metal Industries. Conflicting reports suggest that some STC4/40 vehicles were assembled at Beadle's premises in Kent (or not), although this belief might arise from an observation of the plate carried on some STC4/40s which proclaims the use of Beadle patents in the vehicles' chassisless structures.

Deliveries of production examples began in March 1950 with STC4/40s for Ribble Motor Services (CRN 212) and Boyer of Rothley (GAY 50). By the end of 1950 STC4/40s were in service with Dickson, of Dundee; Wigmore, of Dinnington; Cooper, of Oakengates; Mid-Wales Motorways; and Tor Bus, of Haytor Vale in Devonshire. In addition the company had delivered its first three coach variants, Beadle-bodied SLC4/35s for Davies, of Blackburn (two) and Pitt, of Warrington. This brought the grand total of deliveries during 1950 to 16. There were also no fewer than six UK demonstrators: four STC4/40s (GNT 190, GNT 587, GUJ 457, GUJ 608), an SLC4/35 (GNT 188), and an STC6/44 (GUX 614). There was also an overseas demonstrator, chassis number SLC6/42/34, bringing the total to 23 for the year. It was hardly earth-shaking, but it was a respectable start, and when reports started to come in about overheating engines, Sentinel confidently put it down to teething troubles as one might expect from any new power-plant installation. In light of this the new STC6/44 received its enlarged version of the Ricardo engine without due consideration of alternative engine choices.

Sentinel was out in force at the 1950 Commercial Motor Show, with Earls Court (or the adjacent demonstration park) graced by the presence of STC4/40 GUJ 457 in Cooper, of Oakengates, livery; STC6/44 GUX 614 in pseudo-Ribble livery complete with imaginary fleet number 266; SLC4/35 chassis number 28 in Wigmore, of Dinnington, colours; and Park Royal bodied SLC6/42 chassis number 34, destined for export to Brazil. The STC6/44 demonstrated the peculiarities of Sentinel's numbering system by being chassis number 95 despite being the 23rd vehicle off the line. To all those attending the Show that October it must have seemed that Sentinel were a thriving manufacturer with a fine product range and a healthy customer base.

Sadly, even at this early stage, all was not what it seemed. Of the four exhibits, three could have told another story. STC4/40 GUJ 457 had been intended as the second vehicle for Cooper, with delivery just before Christmas 1950. In the event Cooper became so rapidly disillusioned with their first vehicle that delivery of the second was declined and GUJ

Above: The third prototype also had its bodywork assembled by Beadle but received a Beadle-designed radiator panel to improve its appearance and this became standard on production STC4/40s. **CRN 211** is seen in full Ribble colours (including cream rear dome) but is actually on a test-run through the Shropshire countryside before delivery to the Preston firm. The company vehicle on the right is a DV4 dropside lorry.

Below: The SLC4/35 coach demonstrator, **GNT 188**, with Beadle C35C bodywork. Coach operators were not overly impressed by the styling and several specified the wares of Plaxton and Gurney Nutting in lieu as a condition of purchase. The proposed 30-foot variant, the SLC6/39, was never built due to lack of demand. GNT 188 did the rounds, both as a demonstrator and as a pre-delivery hire vehicle, before sale to Empress Coaches in Bristol.. It went for scrap when barely nine years old after operation by Wessex Coaches' subsidiary Chard and District.

457 remained with Sentinel, in Cooper livery, as a demonstrator until March 1952.

The SLC4/35 coach had a similar pedigree. It was ordered by Wigmore, of Dinnington, to complement their existing STC4/40 bus, but experience with the latter resulted in cancellation before delivery. It ended up with Grainger, of Smethwick. On the overseas front the SLC6/42 had been intended as the first of six for Vicao National in Rio de Janeiro, but no further deliveries to Brazil took place, although one appears to have been delivered to Uruguay at a later date and fitted with local bodywork.

Something was beginning to go wrong, and the problem in almost every case could be blamed on the engine or its mountings. With orders for 1951 deliveries running at more than double the 1950 level it must have been difficult for anyone in the Company to suggest a complete redesign and mouths were kept tightly shut as dozens of DV4 lorries were returned to the dealers for rectification of their overheated powerplants (or worse).

Successes and setbacks

The highlight of 1951 was the delivery of 14 STC6/44s to Ribble, although even this triumph was tempered by the fact that the BET subsidiary had returned to Leyland, ordering Royal Tigers by the hundred. All twenty of Ribble's Sentinels were banished to Carlisle as if they were a reminder of some illicit affair best kept out of sight.

The second biggest order of the year came from a very different operator, Brown, of Donnington Wood in Shropshire, who took five SLC4/35 coaches for use on military leave services from RAF Shawbury and RAF Ternhill. In later years they would be adapted for bus work and used on the operator's services in Telford New Town. Further south the Bristol Co-operative Society (trading as Queen of the Road) took two of the Beadle-bodied coaches while single examples went to Benyon, of Atherton in Lancashire; Grainger, of Smethwick (the aforementioned Show exhibit); Lloyd-Jones Brothers and Pritchard of Narberth (both in western Wales); and Warner, of Tewkesbury in Gloucestershire. An interesting development was the delivery of an SLC4/35 coach with Gurney Nutting bodywork to Domino Coaches, of Barry, perhaps suggesting that the standard Beadle body was not to everyone's taste.

It was the best year for the SLC4/35, with fourteen produced (thirteen sales plus an updated demonstrator) and the last good year for the STC4/40, with a pair delivered to local operator Corvedale, of Ludlow, and single examples to Edwards Brothers, of Crymmych; Harries, of Prendergast; Mid-Wales Motorways; Morrison, of Tenby; and Roberts, of Newport (all in Wales); as well as to Connor and Graham, of Easington in the East Riding of Yorkshire; Moffitt, of Acomb (Northumberland); Smith, of Trench (another local Shropshire operator); and K.W. Services, of Daventry (Northamptonshire). These were mainly family-owned rural enterprises and few would ever order more than one new bus at a time.

The larger version of the bus, the indisputably handsome STC6/44, with its lantern windscreen and transatlantic ambience, did best of all in 1951 with eighteen being produced. Fourteen were for Ribble, one for Boyer, of Rothley (who had previously taken an STC4/40); one for Duggins' Princess Bus Service, of Newcastle-under-Lyme; and two for use as demonstrators. At the end of 1951 Sentinel had an astounding total of nine demonstrators: three STC6/44s (GUX 614, HAW 577 and HAW 578); four STC4/40s (GNT 190, GNT 587, GUJ 457 and GUJ608); and two SLC4/35s (GNT 188 and HNT 101). Not all were in use at any given time but, with total sales at this point barely scraping 60, it was undoubtedly excessive. By the start of 1952 Sentinel's management had been forced to accept that remedial action was necessary.

Desperate measures

With the Ribble order completed and no further prospect of orders from the BET Group because of Sentinel being omitted from the list of approved suppliers, it was clear that a change of direction was necessary on almost every level. Orders for 1952 were less than half that of the previous year (19 rather than 40), which still represented a decrease even if the Ribble STC6/44s are removed from the 1951 figures. The reason was simple: Sentinels were

Above: We have been unable to find a shot of the first STC6/44 (GUX 614) in demonstration livery (i.e. Ribble), but here is its successor **HUJ 619** in the vehicle park at the 1952 Commercial Motor Show alongside a Duple-bodied Bedford SB. After the decision to terminate the STC4 and STC6 models HUJ 619 was sold to Whieldon's Green Bus, Rugeley, and later saw service with Riviera in Cornwall before conversion into a stock-car transporter.

Below: Intended as the first of six SLC6/42 vehicles for Viacao National in Brazil, this was in fact the only one to reach that country. Its identity there has proven elusive and this photograph is of little assistance as it was taken at the premises of Park Royal who built the 42-seat dual-doorway bodywork. It appeared at the 1950 Commercial Motor Show, still in anonymous form, before export to Brazil.

acquiring a reputation for unreliability, both as lorries and as buses. The time had come to bite the bullet and do something to improve the engines. This improvement was largely concerned with removing the Ricardo 'Comet' air-cell combustion chamber and adapting the engine block to take conventional direct-injection equipment. In this updated format the engines were originally known as 4SRH2 and 6SRH2 according to their number of cylinders, but these labels were soon discarded in favour of the simpler (and less evocative) 4D and 6D. In theory the indirect injection variant remained available, but in practice none were built after April 1952.

The redesign was an expensive business, but Sentinel doubled this expense by offering to convert any existing engines to the new specification - free of charge to those in possession of a factory warranty. This was a generous offer and was immediately taken up by most Sentinel bus operators. It was hoped that this gesture would restore confidence in the marque.

The second major change came with a round of cost-cutting measures which included reducing the demonstration fleet from nine to four. Two of the STC4/40s were sold to Richardson (Majestic), of Thorne in Yorkshire; and another to Maryland Coaches, of London E15. SLC4/35 prototype GNT 188 went to Empress Coaches in Bristol, STC6/44 GUX 614 was sold to Llynfi Motors, of Maesteg, and STC6/44 HAW 577 went to Camplejohn Brothers, the well-known Yorkshire independent, who also acquired a brand-new vehicle at the same time.

Other sales of new STC6/44s during 1952 were to Davies Brothers, of Pencader; Edwards Brothers, of Crymmych; and Roberts, of Newport (all in western Wales, the latter two with STC4/40s already in their fleets); Simmons, of Great Gonerby in Lincolnshire (trading as Reliance); and Owen, of Upper Boddington in Northamptonshire, who took a vehicle with a Nottinghamshire registration originally intended for Leon, of Finningley (another cancelled order).

General dissatisfaction with the under-powered, fire-prone, STC4/40 was shown by a complete absence of UK orders. Two vehicles were earmarked as European demonstrators (chassis numbers STC4/40/17 and 18) and the latter at least made it to the Netherlands where it dropped its engine while being demonstrated to a potential client. It returned in shame to Shrewsbury and conversion of chassis number 17 to left-hand drive was discreetly abandoned. The only four-cylinder buses actually sold during 1952 (apart from former demonstrators) were four STC4/Es shipped to Singapore for automotive distributor George Lee and resold to local operators.

On the coaching front, only two Beadle-bodied SLC4/35s were delivered, one each to existing customers Grainger, of Smethwick, and the Bristol Co-op. Gurney Nutting produced its second (and last) coach body on an SLC4/35 - this time for Thomas, of North Muskham near Newark, while Plaxton produced their first for Sentinel distributor (and coach operator) Wiggs Grey Coaches, London SE15. Plaxton bodied two further SLC4/35s during 1952, one built speculatively for Wiggs in anticipation of their first demonstrator achieving a rapid sale (it didn't, and the unwanted Venturer remained at Scarborough until 1954) and the other built to the order of Sentinel's West Bromwich distributor who eventually sold it in the spring of 1953.

From 1951 Sentinel had also offered a 30ft coach model for the UK market, the SLC6/39, but this had found no takers - possibly because of its Beadle bodywork. In late 1952 the 30ft coaches finally materialised, albeit in a hybrid form which involved using the running units from unsold STC6/44s adapted to fit 'outside' bodywork. The first of these, designated as an SLC6/41, was delivered to Warners, of Tewkesbury, carrying a Plaxton Venturer 41-seat centre-entrance body, while the second appeared at the 1952 Commercial Motor Show with a Bellhouse-Hartwell Landmaster body painted in the livery of Smiths, of Wigan. In the event Smiths decided against the purchase of

*Right: Silent reliable power in the shape of STC4/40 **AYJ 822**, operated on local services in Dundee by Dicksons (thus the bridge in the background). This vehicle too migrated to Cornwall for use by Mundy (Silver Queen) and then passed from them to Fenland operator Pooley, of Long Sutton.*

any Sentinels and the vehicle was sold to Blue Cars, the London-based coach operator which specialised in European tours. It carried a chassis-plate proclaiming it to be an SLC6/44, but this was a mistake. Blue Cars also acquired a left-hand drive SLC6/42, originally intended for export to Argentina, and fitted it with a very similar Bellhouse-Hartwell body. Completed SLC6/42 exports were limited to two for Portugal which later suffered the indignity of being rebuilt with Leyland engines.

In effect Sentinel was having a sale of all its unwanted stock, attempting to turn as many assets as possible into hard cash to help pay for the engine redesign and rebuild programme. Despite this refocussing it all proved to be too much for some of the major distributors who found more reliable brands to sell to their customers. Some of Sentinel's own sales team followed suit, leaving the besieged company with a shattered dealer network and a brand new sales force taking over in the middle of a crisis. Surprisingly, the morale of the new personnel was high, as the board of Metal Industries had agreed to another influx of capital for a relaunch of the bus and coach range. It had, however, been made perfectly clear that this represented the company's last chance.

Sentinel Mark Two

Sentinel had produced a total of 24 vehicles during 1952, 19 of which were delivered to customers; the remainder were: two SLC4/35s unsold at Plaxtons, two STC4/40s intended for Europe, and a new STC6/44 demonstrator, HUJ 619. The following year was to be even worse with production down to single figures. The collapse of the sales and dealer operations had been largely responsible; another factor was the redevelopment of the production line to handle an entirely new model targeted specifically at coach operators. This emerged in early 1953 as the SLC6/30, the final part of the designator now indicating the length in feet rather than the seating capacity. The new sales force received a positive reaction from potential customers and the first few orders began to trickle in for 1954 delivery.

The eight vehicles actually produced during 1953 were a mixed bag and most represented a second phase of the clearance sale. One of the SLC4/35s in storage at Plaxtons was sold to Horton, of West Bromwich, and an SLC6/42 was shipped to Ceylon. JNT 763 was a new STC6/44 demonstrator, replacing HUJ 619; the latter was sold to Wheildon's Green Bus, of Rugeley in Staffordshire, along with the first built and last remaining STC4/40 demonstrator, GNT 190, and a trio of 'new' STC6/44s which were registered as YRF 732-4. The exact purchase price for these five vehicles remained confidential, but was rumoured to be so low that Green Bus made a profit when it sold them four years later. A similarly generous deal led to Boyer, of Rothley, increasing its Sentinel fleet to three with the purchase of former STC6/44 demonstrator HAW 578, while STC4/40 JUJ 264 (the machine which dropped its engine in the Netherlands) was sold to Brown, of Donnington Wood, still without its engine. It is believed that Browns fitted it with a spare, bought with their SLC4/35 coaches, which had not yet been needed.

The seventh and eighth vehicles produced during 1953 were the most important ones, being of the new SLC6/30 variant designed to save the company. Chassis number 6301 was used (without bodywork) for testing purposes, and was eventually sold in South Africa as the basis of a pantechnicon van. The second vehicle, number 6302, received a Plaxton Venturer 39-seat centre-entrance body and was delivered to Partridge (Bantam Coaches) of Coventry in March 1953 for a period of in-service evaluation. Sentinel was almost ready for its second assault on the marketplace.

The logic of this make or break attack appeared impeccable. The large stage-carriage operators seemed forever out of Sentinel's reach after the initial euphoria surrounding the Ribble order. Although BET subsidiary Maidstone and District had tried an STC6/44 during 1952 (probably as a result of their relationship with John C Beadle), this produced no change in the Group's purchasing policy, which was becoming slightly stricter than it had been in the immediate postwar years. In the independent sector the few really large operators (Barton, LUT, and West Riding) had already tried the demonstrators and then placed orders elsewhere. Sentinel's existing customers for STC bus models were small operators and

Above: The second Brazilian vehicle went to Uruguay, the third and fourth to Portugal where the latter is seen sporting its original 30-seat coach body built by Portuguese company P. and F. Crespo. Registered as **BL-18-52** by Isadore Duarte it later lost this magnificent body and was rebuilt as a dual-purpose vehicle with the added insult of a Leyland engine in place of its Sentinel 6SRH unit.

Below: The SLC6/42 was designed as an exclusively export model for 33-foot bodywork, but one found a career with London-based Blue Cars as **MYV 637**. Given length restrictions at that time the vehicle required special permits in the UK and therefore spent most of its working life based at Boulogne. It is seen here at the 1952 Commercial Motor Show, displaying its eccentric Bellhouse-Hartwell Landmaster body (complete with toilet) to an astonished public.

unlikely to yield more than a handful of repeat orders. Logic dictated that the company should concentrate on the buoyant coaching sector and give a low priority to further service bus developments.

A revamped dealer network came into operation in the autumn of 1953 with the new emphasis on coaches in mind. Wilkes and Meade, the Leeds-based dealer and coachbuilder, which had previously had little success with its Sentinel agency, had been absorbed by the Wallace Arnold group and the name of the prestigious (and enormous) tour operator undoubtedly helped to raise the SLC6/30s profile among smaller Yorkshire operators. In similar vein, the Middlesex coachbuilder James Whitson became a dealer and also undertook to produce STC6/44 clone bodywork on the new SLC6/30 chassis for any repeat (or indeed new) customers who wanted a Sentinel bus. Surprisingly perhaps, Whitson were perfectly willing to accept orders for Sentinel coaches with bodywork by their neighbours at Duple, although they naturally preferred that customers should order their own Grand Prix body style. Sentinel's other regional dealerships, such as K & B in Newcastle, appeared to actively encourage the selection of Whitson bodywork in areas where it had previously been little known.

As orders for the SLC6/30 reached respectable levels the management and staff at Shrewsbury hoped for better days in 1954. To help the cash flow, a final part of the clearance sale took place. A deal was done with the owner of major County Durham independent operator Trimdon Motor Services which involved no fewer than ten vehicles, two of them brand-new SLC6/30 coaches with A.C.B. Coronation Land Cruiser bodywork (PPT 690/850), the rest a rag-bag of bargain basement leftovers comprising JNT 763, the STC6/44 demonstrator (which Trimdon reregistered as OUP 578), the undelivered European STC4/40 demonstrator JUX 270 (which became OUP 581), three unsold STC4/40s (OUP 579, 580 and 582), an unsold Beadle-bodied SLC4/35 (PPT 212), and two Beadle-bodied SLC4/27s (PPT 213/4). These latter vehicles represented an attempt by Sentinel to use up the significant quantity of SLC4/35 components still present at Shrewsbury and Dartford. They were clearly of the old and widely unloved design and apart from the Trimdon machines only two were sold.

The full-price deliveries for the year included two SLC6/30s for the Bristol Co-op's Queen of the Road fleet (one with Plaxton Venturer bodywork, the other a Whitson Grand Prix), another two for Lewis, of Greenwich (both with Duple Elizabethan bodies), and single examples of the SLC6/30 coach for Longstaff, of Morpeth in Northumberland, and Hastelow of Malvern (both Whitson Grand Prix); for Bluebird, of Weymouth (Duple Elizabethan); and for Bluebird Garages, of Kingston-upon-Hull (Plaxton Venturer). The latter was delivered via Wallace Arnold and they also took a Burlingham Seagull bodied demonstrator (SUG 19) which was rapidly resold to Metcalfe, of Keighley. Whitson also delivered an SLC6/30 bus to Simmons, of Great Gonerby, to match their existing genuine STC6/44 in Reliance livery.

Two new demonstrators were produced to help flaunt the company's updated wares. KUJ 141, the coach model, had conventional Duple Elizabethan bodywork, but there was also a new bus model, KUX 412, with unusual dual-door bodywork by A.C.B. In fact, just as Sentinel were conceding the lack of opportunity in the stage-carriage market, several bodybuilders were looking at the SLC6/30 and seeing it as the basis for a service bus. As well as Whitson and A.C.B., Burlingham produced one for Whieldon's Green Bus, built to the Blackpool company's standard 44-seat front-entrance design.

This vehicle (775 ERF) was one of six Sentinels which laid siege to visitors at the 1954 Commercial Motor Show. The others were the Burlingham Seagull-bodied SUG 19 (by then in Metcalfe livery), chassis number 63013 with Duple Elizabethan bodywork in Lewis, of Greenwich, livery (it would become PXE 761 in the New Year); chassis number 63017 carrying an STC6-clone body by Whitson and painted in the colour scheme of Draytonian Coaches, of Yiewsley (Whitson's local operator - in the event it was never delivered to them but went to Warners of Tewkesbury as SDF 17); chassis number 63022 with Burlingham Seagull bodywork in Wallace Arnold livery (replacing SUG 19 as their

*Around the same time the SLC4/35 with Beadle coach bodywork was quietly dropped from Sentinel's trade advertisements and replaced by images of Sentinel coaches wearing Plaxton and Gurney Nutting bodywork. The vehicles shown are an SLC6/41 with Plaxton Venturer bodywork (**LDF 296** for Warners of Tewkesbury) and an SLC4/35 with Gurney Nutting C35C bodywork (**LNY 307** for Domino of Barry).*

demonstrator and later registered UUB 931); and chassis number 63023 with 41-seat Whitson Grand Prix bodywork resplendent in the livery of Cowell Brothers, Sunderland. It never operated with them despite the impressive splash it made at Earls Court and ended up being sold to Best and Son, of Wembley (another of Whitson's local operators) as 657 CMT.

Nobody could have tried harder, but Sentinel's logic proved ultimately to be flawed. They had reasoned that small coach operators would be more receptive to the SLC6/30 than would the large group companies, as they frequently changed suppliers from one delivery to the next and had already embraced relatively unconventional designs such as the Commer Avenger without protest. They were also more inclined to chance their arm on less common engine types, with the advantages afforded to the large operators by economy of scale replaced by a mixture of doggedness and ingenuity when dealing with all things mechanical. Sadly the world was changing, even in the back street premises of local private-hire operators and the economics of operating a rare type compared poorly with those of a better-known vehicle. And the SLC6/30 had lost many of the unique selling points of its predecessors.

Direct injection, while improving the engines from a serviceability viewpoint, had also made them noisier while doing little to improve the type's thirstiness for fuel. The modifications had made the Sentinel into a heavier vehicle to the point where it weighed more than one of Leyland's new Tiger Cubs and about the same as an AEC Reliance. For those customers who wanted an underfloor chassis but were averse to AEC's notoriously unreliable AH410 engine or Leyland's fraught-sounding O.350, there were (by 1954) Gardner-powered alternatives including the Atkinson Alpha and Guy Arab UF/LUF. Sentinel's reputation for engine production made the Gardner a clear winner for most potential customers, for all its faults as a coach power-plant.

On top of all this, the market for underfloor-engined vehicles as a whole was being relentlessly corroded by the triumphant advance of the Bedford SB, with the Duple-bodied versions becoming as ubiquitous as their OB/Vista forebears. Variety was plentiful and Sentinel failed to stand out.

The final twelve months

In January 1955 the Board of the Metal Industries group decided to call it a day and Sentinel's sales-force and distributors were told to accept no further orders for diesel lorries, buses, and coaches. Operators with outstanding orders on the books were apprised of the situation and given the alternative of cancellation at no cost if they so chose. As in the engine crisis of 1952 the company continued to act with a sense of honour that eluded many contemporary businesses.

All of the orders which stayed in place were for coach-bodied SLC6/30s. Simmons, of Great Gonerby, bought the final Whitson Grand Prix bodied example, JTL 469, bringing their Sentinel fleet to three. The remaining seven were all equipped with Burlingham Seagull bodywork, four for Schofield, of Marsden near Huddersfield; one for Benyon, of Atherton (who operated it alongside two Beadle-bodied SLC4/35s); and two which had been ordered by Wallace Arnold but were declined upon completion. One of these became the last Sentinel public service vehicle to leave Shrewsbury when it was registered to Bengry (Primrose), of Leominster, in April 1956 as NVJ 664. Other odds and ends disposed of during the final year were the last SLC4/27, which went to Chapple, of Raglan in Monmouthshire; and Whitson's STC6-bodied SLC6/30 bus demonstrator from the 1954 Show, which had previously operated on trade plates but now became SDF 17 with Warner, of Tewkesbury - they were already operating an SLC4/35, an SLC6/41, and the former Maryland Coaches STC4/40.

During 1956 the works was gradually cleared of all trace of the diesel-powered vehicles and by the time Rolls-Royce took over at the end of the year little remained. The manufacturing rights for Sentinel's designs passed to a Warrington-based consortium headed by Tom Ward. Mr Ward, a former haulier, was the owner of North Cheshire Motors, which had been a successful distributor of Sentinel lorries and a less successful

Above: Also at the 1952 Show, this vehicle is an SLC6/41, a model assembled from STC6/44 components to serve as a stop-gap 30ft-long coach in place of the friendless SLC6/39. Another Bellhouse-Hartwell Landmaster, it appeared in the plain cream livery of Smiths, of Wigan, but never ran for them. Instead it was sold to Blue Cars as **NLR 850** and mainly used for premium private-hire work. Its typical outing took it to Brighton or Southend, unlike its more glamorous cousin in Boulogne which ranged as far afield as Greece.

Below: After the 1953 decision to concentrate on the SLC6/30 coach model, it was intended that residual demand for service buses would be met by Whitson, using STC6/44 body panels atop an SLC6/30 chassis. Whieldon's Green Bus preferred to use Burlingham, which resulted in **775 ERF** appearing at the 1954 Commercial Motor Show. It lasted for barely three years before sale to Camplejohn Brothers in Yorkshire, but was caught in service on the Hednesford route before its departure to Barnsley.

27

distributor of Sentinel PSVs (he managed to sell three SLC4/35s in the early days of production). His new company, Transport Vehicles Warrington, acquired a job lot of Sentinel components and used them to manufacture around 100 TVW lorries in the late 1950s, many of them similar in appearance to contemporary ERF products as both manufacturers used the same Congleton based company to manufacture their cab mouldings. TVW also acquired three complete 6-cylinder bus chassis, but these were of the SLC6/33 model and could be completed only as goods vehicles under UK regulations as they then stood. Sadly TVW produced no buses of their own, and by 1961 had followed Sentinel into oblivion.

Rolls-Royce showed little regard for Sentinel's records - this was 1956, long before the general advent of the corporate archive - and all had been discarded by the time anyone thought to ask. Steam-waggon enthusiasts among the Shrewsbury work-force ensured that a passable amount of data on such vehicles survived, but all of the diesel records appear to have ended up as waste-paper. Much of the information presented in this book has been pieced together from widely scattered jigsaw pieces, many of which are still missing. Much has disappeared without trace, including several chassis recorded as exported but never observed in the destination country.

The products of Sentinel are well represented in the ranks of preserved vehicles and, with no fewer than nine diesel PSVs surviving in varying conditions of repair, the company has a fitting monument. They may well have been less than perfect, but they were pioneers and they had style, and will long be remembered by those with an interest in the history of the bus industry. Sentinel remains a name which evokes nostalgia fifty years after the last new vehicle took to the road from the Shrewsbury works.

TECHNICAL DATA

Sentinel's first postwar diesel vehicles were designed for use as lorries and bore entirely logical designations such as DV4/4 (which indicated a Diesel Vehicle with a 4-cylinder engine and four wheels - any doubling of rear wheels was ignored) and DV6T/8 (a 6-cylinder diesel chassis adapted to take tipper bodywork on four axles).

The initial bus prototypes were registered as SB4/40s, translating as Sentinel-Beadle, 4-cylinder bus with 40 seats, but production vehicles emerged as STC4/40s. There is still some controversy about the meaning of the letters STC, which on the original drawings for the type were an abbreviation for Sentinel Transit Coach - engineers from both Ricardo and Chrysler were involved in the design and used their native terminology. However, it seems that this was too vulgarly transatlantic for Sentinel's marketing department, who promptly invented the term Sentinel Town and Country to use in their advertising and sales brochures. Neither definition entered popular usage.

The STC4/40 was soon joined by a 30 feet long, 8 feet wide, 44-seat variant with a 6-cylinder version of the Sentinel-Ricardo engine. This logically became the STC6/44. The range was completed by the Sentinel Luxury Coach versions, the SLC4/35 with the four-cylinder engine and Beadle 35-seat bodywork, and the SLC6/39 with the 6-cylinder and a Beadle superstructure with room for 39. The last of these fell victim to both the engine problems and a general dissatisfaction with the styling of the SLC4/35, and was never actually produced.

On offer for export was the SLC6/42 - a six-cylinder chassis designed to receive locally-built 33ft x 8ft bodywork. The initial order came from a Brazilian operator who chose Park Royal in London as bodybuilder and had the chassis equipped with 42 seats (and room for many standees), thus the final number in the model designator. Recognising that some overseas operators would require shorter vehicles, Sentinel developed export versions of the home-market models which basically differed from their British cousins in being receptive to conventional styles of bodywork. These were designated as STC4/E etc., but this did not appear on their construction plates, where they were described as STC4/40 and so on despite their additional framing and (usually) left-hand drive.

It should perhaps be mentioned at this point that we have chosen to use the model

28

Above: This SLC6/30 with Whitson Grand Prix bodywork appeared at the 1954 Show in the livery of Cowell, Sunderland, but remained in the London area with Best and Sons, of Wembley, as **657 CMT**. Best were understandably proud of this stylish vehicle and entered it in several coach rallies. This is Brighton, but the year remains uncertain.

Below: Another of the 1954 Show participants was Duple Elizabethan-bodied SLC6/30 **PXE 761**, originally ordered by Wiggs but diverted to Lewis, of Greenwich, who operated it in this attractive red, maroon and cream livery. The vehicle survives, largely as a result of its conversion into a stock-car transporter.

29

designators in the oblique-stroke format favoured in most company documents. On the construction plates these were omitted, so vehicle SLC4/35/33 for example (HAW 374) carries SLC4 35 33 on its Sentinel identity plate. On the same vehicle, however, the Beadle plate on the underframe shows their number (JCB 127) and SLC4/35/33.

It seems that Beadle was more careful about the accuracy of these than Sentinel themselves: SLC4/35/23 (HNT 101 - built as a demonstrator) left the works with a plate proclaiming it to be STC4 40 23, while similar machine NLG 176 (the North Cheshire Motors demonstrator) went forth as STC4 40 29. We have corrected these in our listings of vehicles and operators as they are clearly wrong.

Another obvious error occurred on the construction plate of NLR 850, which was described as SLC6 44 102. This was actually one of two 30ft x 8ft coaches manufactured from STC6/44 parts and correctly described as SLC6/41s - a stop-gap model which existed briefly between the phantom SLC6/39 and the later SLC6/30. This error has also been corrected in the vehicle listing with an appropriate footnote.

The second wave

As part of the rehabilitation of the Sentinel name in 1953, the type designators were amended to reflect nominal length rather than the much vaguer factor of recommended seating capacity. By this time the STC4 and STC6 had been dropped from future production plans, but the SLC4/35 was still available and metamorphosed into the SLC4/27 at the nominal expense of six of its inches. It was basically the same ugly duckling and only four were built. Their chassis plates showed their identity in a slightly different format, with NWO 122 being 4271 which indicated SLC4/27 No. 1. The same logic was pursued with the new 30ft x 8ft SLC6/30 chassis with SLC6/30 No. 9 being described as 6309, No. 10 as 63010, and so on. The export model SLC6/42 became the SLC6/33 in this rebranding exercise, but none found bus work; four became brewery wagons in Australia and the remaining three went to TVW to become HGVs in the UK.

One mystery that remains to be explained is the SLC4/30 which was registered in Ceylon (now Sri Lanka) as IC 2191 in 1954 and allegedly fitted with local bodywork to seat 56. This seems to have been assembled from leftover SLC4/35 components, but even had it had considerably extended overhang sections at front and rear it seems unlikely that its seating capacity could have exceeded that of its predecessor, a 33ft-long SLC6/42, which had seating for only 49 (and both vehicles are reported as dual-door with bus seating). We suspect that the total of 56 may have include standing passengers.

In another one-off variation from the production-line standard, STC6/44/91 (HAW 578) was fitted with a Sentinel four-cylinder engine at some point in its early career as a demonstrator, technically turning it into an STC4/44 although there are no reports that the manufacturer's plate was physically altered. Sold by Sentinel to Boyer, of Rothley, it later passed to Midland Red and had adequate power for the terrain around Leicester. Another conversion was that of STC6/44/94 (NNN 998) which had its six-cylinder engine replaced by a four-cylinder while in the possession of a dealer and subsequently operated in this configuration until the end of its career. Again, we have no evidence that the plate was changed to reflect the smaller powerplant.

The sharp-eyed and knowledgable will notice that we have eschewed the model designator SOT6/42, used in some earlier publications for first series vehicles numbers 36 and 37, exported to Portugal. A footnote to the individual vehicle histories explains this. We have been unable to find any contemporary verification of this model, and the vehicles involved appear to be standard SLC6/42s in every regard. In later life both of these buses had their Sentinel 6D engines replaced by Leyland O.600 units and it is possible that the SOT6 designator was applied locally in Portugal, but this is conjecture. The vehicles expired long ago, so examination of the physical evidence is no longer possible. Curiously, the 33ft-long chassis used as the basis of a cattle waggon (chassis number 6336) is also described as an SOT6 in UK tax records.

The table that follows (see page 32) lists the major production models, the STC4/40,

Two Noteworthy Whitson Models!

The Model illustrated alongside is yet another example of superb design by Whitsons. It is a 44-seater service bus on a Sentinel underfloor engine chassis.

Alongside is illustrated the new 41-seater Full Luxury Coach, built on an A.E.C. chassis. Here, indeed, the keynote is elegance, and the beauty of line for which Whitson Coaches are distinguished has never been more pleasingly carried out. In common with all Whitson models, it has large luggage accommodation, air conditioning, heating, radio and the patent Flush-fitting Sliding Door.

James WHITSON & Co., Ltd.
YIEWSLEY · WEST DRAYTON · MIDDLX.
Telephones: West Drayton 2863 & 2953

*A Whitson advertisement showing an SLC6/30 with STC6-style service-bus bodywork (**HCT 618** of Simmons) and an unidentified AEC Reliance with Grand Prix luxury coach bodywork. Whitson were more enthusiastic about Sentinel chassis than most of their regular customers who preferred the Reliance or Leyland's Tiger Cub.*

VEHICLE SPECIFICATIONS

MODEL	STC4/40	STC6/44	SLC4/35	SLC6/42	SLC6/30
Nominal Length	27ft 6ins	30ft 0ins	27ft 6ins	33ft 0ins	30ft 0ins
Nominal Width	7ft 6ins	8ft 0ins	7ft 6ins	8ft 0ins	8ft 0 ins
Wheelbase	14ft 9ins	15ft 7ins	14ft 9ins	18ft 4 ins	15ft 7ins
Max. Gross Weight	21,168 lbs	21,168 lbs	21,168 lbs	28,000 lbs	23,520 lbs
Engine Type	4SRH*	6SRH +	4SRH *	6SRH	6SRH2
Gearbox	5-speed	4 or 5-speed	5-speed	5-speed	4 or 5-speed
Brakes	Hydraulic	Vacuum	Hydraulic	Vacuum	Vacuum

NOTES:- * Most (but not all) retrofitted to 4SRH2 specification in 1952
+ Early production examples retrofitted to 6SRH2 specification in 1952
Later vehicles fitted with 6SRH2 engines from new

ENGINE SPECIFICATIONS

MODEL	4SRH	4SRH2 (4D)	6SRH	6SRH2 (6D)
Cylinders	4	4	6	6
Capacity	6.08 litres	6.08 litres	9.12 litres	9.12 litres
Injection	Indirect	Direct	Indirect	Direct
Output (in BHP)	90 @ 2000 RPM	80 @ 1800 RPM	135 @ 2000 RPM	120 @ 1800 RPM

STC6/44, SLC4/35, SLC6/42 and SLC6/30. Nominal external dimensions may not apply to individual vehicles, particularly in the case of the SLC4/35s with Plaxton bodywork. All three of these were 37-seaters, a capacity achieved by extending the superstructure to 29ft 2ins; two of the three were built to a width of eight feet rather than 7ft 6ins. Those were the days of bespoke bodybuilding and the customer got what he asked for.

Bodywork analysis

Of the 146 diesel PSV chassis built by Sentinel between 1948 and 1956, 17 were built for export and a further four were completed in HGV configuration for the UK market. The balance of 125 vehicles received PSV bodywork by nine different manufacturers. In the table on the opposite page, for brevity, the entrance position and seating capacity are given as codes, familiar to many enthusiasts, which are explained in full in the section dealing with individual vehicle histories.

In total there were 63 four-cylinder vehicles and 62 six-cylinder machines, with 69 chassis being sold as buses (including one dual-purpose vehicle) and 56 as coaches. In addition there were ten export chassis which received PSV bodywork (one by Park Royal in Britain, the remainder locally), resulting in a grand total of 135 Sentinel buses and coaches.

WHAT THE PAPERS SAID

Press reaction to the public debut of the Sentinel-Beadle at 1948's Commercial Motor Show was universally positive. Then, as now, the transport press was obsessed with the new and innovative, and in 1948 the SB4/40 was cutting edge technology. Midland Red's pioneering work with underfloor engined single-deckers had whetted the industry's appetite for larger-capacity vehicles, and Sentinel had beaten Leyland to market by almost two years.

True, Sentinel was an unknown quantity, even when compared with Foden or Thornycroft, but the market was booming in the early postwar years and it must have seemed highly probable that such innovative enterprise would meet with success.

Debut of a pioneer

"Undoubtedly one of the most unusual vehicles was the Sentinel-Beadle ... one of a fleet ordered by the Western National Omnibus Company. The vehicle, by virtue of its construction and design, has been brought down to the remarkably low unladen weight of 5 tons 8 cwts. Because of this, and the great saving in space achieved by the underfloor design, it has been possible to seat 40 passengers and yet still conform to Ministry of Transport requirements.

	Four-cylinder	
SB4/40	Beadle B40F	3
STC4/40	Sentinel B40F	31
SLC4/35	Beadle C35C	20
SLC4/35	Gurney Nutting C35C	2
SLC4/35	Plaxton Venturer C37C	3
SLC4/27	Beadle C35C	4

	Six-cylinder	
STC6/44	Sentinel B44F	30
SLC6/41	Bellhouse Hartwell Landmaster C32C	1
SLC6/41	Plaxton Venturer C41C	1
SLC6/42	Bellhouse Hartwell Landmaster C32CT	1
SLC6/30	A.C.B. Coronation Land Cruiser C41C	2
SLC6/30	A.C.B. B40D	1
SLC6/30	Burlingham Seagull Mk II C37C/C41C	5
SLC6/30	Burlingham Seagull Mk III C41C	4
SLC6/30	Burlingham B44F	1
SLC6/30	Duple Elizabethan C41C	5
SLC6/30	Plaxton Venturer C37C/C41C	3
SLC6/30	Whitson Grand Prix C37C/C40C/C41C	5
SLC6/30	Whitson B44F/DP44F	3

The Show vehicle has a service bus body but we understand that other designs include luxury versions which still allow 37 passengers to be seated.

The interior of the bus has been kept very spacious by eliminating window-pans and mounting the windows directly into their frames by using the Beclawart design of rubber beading fed from a gun.

The body is entirely of all-metal construction with the exception of the wood flooring. The underfloor engine is a new model designed by Sentinel (Shrewsbury) Limited. It is a four-cylinder unit which develops 90 bhp at 2000 rpm and has a maximum torque of 255 ft lbs at 1500 rpm; it has three-point suspension on rubber insulated mountings.

We had a run in one of these vehicles which was operating outside the Show and were very impressed by the liveliness of the engine, its silence, and private-car performance. Overseas buyers were interested in the 5-speed gearbox with an overspeed top gear which enables the vehicle to cruise most successfully at speeds of some 60 mph." *(Passenger Transport, 15th October 1948)*

As mentioned previously, there never was a fleet for Western National. HOD 57, the vehicle on display inside at the 1948 Show, was merely an experiment for the nationalised company, an afterthought to an order for twelve throwaway Bedford-Beadles. The reference to the engine mountings is interesting in light of subsequent difficulties, as is the assertion of top speeds up to 60 mph. Reaction to this claim among those familiar with four-cylinder Sentinels can be guaranteed to include laughter and hoots of derision. The vehicle referred to as giving demonstration rides outside the Show can only have been EUJ 792.

Road test in the west country

"The route traversed during the first part of the test run provided everything one could desire for evaluating the qualities of Beadle construction from the passenger angle, and I was greatly impressed by the smooth motion,

the absence of fore and aft pitch when uneven road surfaces were traversed, as well as perfect cornering stability. There is nothing even remotely resembling metallic resonance within the saloon which gives one the feeling of being driven over a rubberised road when, in fact, the surface is no better than it ought to be. Though much nearer to the engine than in buses of conventional layout, passengers have no aural evidence of the fact for, when pulling steadily, the power unit is commendably quiet.

Another commendable feature demonstrated by the tests was the smooth transmission of engine power through the gears, propeller-shaft, and final drive, even under the very exacting conditions imposed for the final test, for rolling acceleration from 10-30 mph when all the chassis units are pre-loaded and pre-stressed to a high degree at the start. Incidentally, it may be mentioned that the tests provided further evidence of easy riding in the Beadle bus in that the movements were unusually steady, by contrast with other vehicles in such conditions.

Efforts to obtain maximum passenger accommodation have somewhat restricted the dimensions of the driving compartment, the back of the driving seat being only 17 inches from the rim of the steering wheel. Vision through the full-fronted windscreen is good, the driver having a clear view of the nearside through the conveniently arranged front entrance. Like the rest of the bus, the driver's compartment is comfortable, quiet, and free from draughts. Notwithstanding the unusual position of the power unit, Beadle designers have managed to overcome front suspension problems associated with this particular form of bus layout, and the driver gets full benefit from the well-proportioned and resilient springs which also absorb shocks that otherwise might reach the steering wheel.

The remainder of the 42-miles test trip served to confirm the generally good impression of this very useful type of bus which, from a constructional point of view, incorporates many desirable features too numerous to describe adequately in a road test report." *(Passenger Transport, 13th May 1949)*

The vehicle involved in this test was Western National's HOD 57 and the test run took place in the vehicle's home area between Sidmouth and Taunton. Note that the writer refers to the vehicle as a Beadle throughout, emphasising the fact that Western National's familiarity was with the Kent bodybuilder rather than with Sentinel. It could also be that WNOC personnel preferred to classify the machine as a Beadle to head off inevitable comparisons with the Sentinel steam-waggons still used by many small West Country hauliers at that time.

The view from 'Bus And Coach'

"In broad outline the Sentinel bus is of the pattern having sufficient forward overhang to permit the provision of an entrance at the extreme front end of the nearside. Thus, full use can be made of the area alongside the driver, which has been freed by taking the engine from its traditional position and mounting it beneath the floor. This leaves an unobstructed floor space capable of seating 40 passengers, all in forward-facing pairs of seats at least 2ft 3 ins apart, the floor itself being flat except for shallow wheel-boxes and the emergency exit being in the centre at the back. The driver is positioned at the extreme front end where his vision of the road ahead, and on his near-side, as well as of the entrance, could hardly be better. The comparatively short wheelbase, brought about by the retracted position of the front axle, gives the vehicle a reduced turning circle and, in combination with the disposition of the engine-gearbox unit, a better distribution of weight between the tyres. In appearance too, the vehicle is nicely balanced.

The whole frame structure is notable for its stark simplicity and the economic use of the material employed. It is based upon a rectangular grid-like underframe which, whilst it is stiff enough to allow the vehicle to be run as a 'chassis' and, in fact, to carry a full load of test weights in this form, does derive some additional strength from the superstructure and panels; they complete what is in effect a hollow girder having a high strength to weight ratio. The floor of the bus is laid over the frame grid.

The relative positions of the driver's seat and the entrance alongside one another are naturally suited to a pay-as-you-enter arrangement and when called for it can be provided. Normally, however, the driving

Above: Wallace Arnold inherited a Sentinel dealership with the business of Wilks and Meade. The company's second demonstrator, **UUB 931**, appeared at the 1954 Show with a Burlingham Seagull body, but was soon transferred to the operational tours fleet where it lasted as an odd man out for more than eight years.

Below: Several of the Ribble STC6/44 fleet saw further service as PSVs, but this is the only one known to have received a repaint with its new operator. **DRN 344** is seen in September 1963 when freshly delivered to Sproat, of Bedford (Cedar Coaches), who used it on a schools contract. It later became a mobile snack-bar in the Nottingham area.

compartment is screened from the passenger saloon and a sliding door for the driver is provided on the off-side, and in any case he has an excellent view of passengers boarding and alighting from the bus, and comfortable quarters." *(Bus and Coach, January 1950)*

The verbosity of the report suggests a correspondent being paid by the word, while the final paragraph takes us back to an era when single-crew operation was an innovation yet to be accepted by the workforce. As a result, Sentinel STC4/40s were built with a privacy screen around the driver, and this had to be removed and replaced with a cash-desk door to enable fare collection by the driver.

The voice of optimism

"The Sentinel bus and coach chassis with underfloor engine, announced some months ago, is now in full production and we understand that this model is now available for reasonably early delivery.

The chassis can be fitted with either the Sentinel four-cylinder or six-cylinder underfloor engine, both of which are of the horizontal direct injection type, while other features of the construction include a 5-speed gearbox, giving a wide range of control under all conditions. The new chassis can be constructed in either 7ft 6ins or 8ft widths and the complete vehicle allows comfortable seating for up to 44 passengers.

Both the four-cylinder and six-cylinder engines produced by Sentinel (Shrewsbury) Ltd are noted for their reliability, and an advanced design of engine suspension and springing gives freedom from vibration, together with comfortable riding for the passengers at all speeds.

The underfloor engine has particularly good accessibility features both for inspection and maintenance, whilst the layout results in an almost total lack of noise in the saloon, and the complete elimination of heat and fumes, both in the cab and the saloon.

We understand that Sentinel (Shrewsbury) Ltd offer an open invitation to coachbuilders and fleet owners to visit the Sentinel Works at Shrewsbury at any time to inspect the chassis during the various stages of their manufacture." *(Passenger Transport, 14th May 1952)*

It is quite difficult to equate this report with the true state of affairs at Shrewsbury in the spring of 1952, as reference to earlier pages will reveal. There were certainly no new models on offer at the time - the larger STC6/44 had made its debut some eighteen months before and had already been in service with Ribble for much of the preceding year. The glowing praise for the engines is also hard to rationalise, as the direct-injection versions had only just been introduced (and therefore could hardly be noted for their reliability) while the older versions with indirect injection were notoriously unreliable. The 'advanced design of engine suspension' had also proven highly suspect by this time and resulted in several power units falling out of vehicles in motion.

One suspects that the story began life as a Sentinel press-release and slipped through the critical net during editorial holidays. Or perhaps the staff of Passenger Transport merely felt sorry for the workers in Shrewsbury and allowed them a free plug for their products in the hope that the company would survive.

Engine replacement therapy

"...credit must also be given to Sentinel as the first British vehicle builder to put an underfloor engine chassis on the market - a lorry, it is true, but nevertheless the type under discussion. The makers had not previously made automotive diesel engines and their venture into a new field was courageous, although possibly the flat-engine conception was favoured by there being no vertical engine in production to create a precedent and to be 'converted' to a new location. As originally designed it embodied the Ricardo Comet air-cell combustion chamber, even though the British automotive industry had already indicated its solid preference for direct injection. Sentinel engines have recently been adapted to take direct injection heads, multi-hole sprayers, and toroidal cavity pistons, with a minimum of alterations to existing material, so that either type of combustion system is now available.

The six-cylinder engine is of 9.12 litres capacity which, with the direct injection head, develops 120 bhp at 1800 rpm as compared with the 135 bhp at 2000 rpm of the air-cell type; specific consumption, of course, shows

Above: Ribble's **DRN 350** went to Rodgers, of Redcar (primarily a taxi operator), and was briefly used on a free service to and from a local bingo hall in which Mr Rodgers had an interest. As can be seen it operated in basic Ribble livery without fleetnames.

Below: Beadle-bodied SLC4/35 **PHA 928** started life with Grainger, of Smethwick (Eagle Coaches), but by the time of this June 1964 photograph had moved a few miles to West Bromwich, where it saw service with Collett. Beadle-bodied coaches had a curious variety of front ends to them, almost as if the Kent bodybuilder was making them from leftovers.

the normal improvement associated with direct injection." *(Bus and Coach, 19th November 1952)*

As can be seen, Bus and Coach's version of events was closer to reality but refrained from being overly critical of Sentinel's hard-pressed management. A fleet manager and potential Sentinel-purchaser could read this article and make an informed decision about the continuing viability of the marque, satisfied that the troublesome indirect-injection system was a thing of the past. Nevertheless the figures given demonstrate the 12% loss in performance incurred by the switch to direct injection, while a lack of corresponding exactitude with relation to the alleged improvement in fuel consumption leaves the reader wondering why. The answer appears to be that the improvement in fuel consumption was negligible by comparison to the loss of power. The direct injection equipment also made the vehicles slightly heavier which rapidly eroded any (minimal) increase in fuel efficiency. Potential buyers compared the figures with those of the new lightweight models from AEC, Guy and Leyland and saw no valid reason to turn to Sentinel. The bus industry, even in those heady days of high loadings, was already committed to economics rather than art.

SENTINELS IN SERVICE

Ribble Motor Services kept its Sentinels for more than twelve years, an average lifespan for single-deckers with BET Group companies, although the Ribble Leyland Olympics delivered at the same time as the STC6/44s ran for up to five years longer. The reasons for this were twofold, and neither reflected badly on Sentinel. Firstly, the large numbers of single-deckers bought by Ribble in 1950-4 were destined to be replaced by 36ft-long Leyland Leopards, and these had a later version of the same engine as had the Olympics and Royal Tigers. This offered a much easier engineering transition between types, especially if the parts not shared in common by the older and newer variants of the Leyland O.600 could be stored in spaces previously used for Sentinel parts. Secondly, the surviving Olympics (the last was retired in 1968) had been adapted for driver-only operation in the late 1950s, while the Ribble STC4/40s had retained their privacy screening throughout their careers and thus needed conductors. By the early 1960s they were too old to justify the cost of their conversion.

Furthermore, twelve years working in the Lake District would have taken its toll on the vehicles, particularly as they neared the end of their depreciation period. Whilst well maintained and roadworthy they had encountered far more wear and tear than their cousins in flatter regions of the country. The handful of operators who bought former Ribble STC6/44s found this out the hard way with none of the vehicles lasting for more than a year with a new owner. The STC4/40s fared even worse, with none seeing further use as PSVs and most ending up as site-huts or mobile shops. In fairness, it was a bad time to be buying second-hand Sentinels. After the Rolls-Royce takeover, responsibility for service and support of existing Sentinel diesel vehicles had passed to Tom Ward's TVW syndicate. In 1961 this venture had closed its doors and so any future Sentinel spares would have to come from existing stocks (already dwindling) or from vehicles cannibalised by dealers such as Cowley, Everall, and Hughes. Many of the vehicles seen in those companies' yards at the time may have seemed unattractive to potential buyers, but were in fact deliberately unsold to keep livelier machines on the road. Such was the fate of many of Ribble's once proud fleet of STC buses.

Independent bus fleets

Browns of Donnington Wood, Shropshire, took delivery of five brand new SLC4/35s and supplemented these with two former demonstrators (another SLC4/35 and an STC4/40 bus recovered from an embarrassing adventure in the Netherlands) and a third-hand STC4/40 which had seen service with Maryland in London and Warners in Tewkesbury. Nearly all of these vehicles served the company for more than a twenty year lifespan and Browns were proud enough of them to boast about their 'locally made buses' on signs at bus-shelters and in timetable leaflets. One fortunate side-effect of their late withdrawal was their availability to the

Above: Gurney Nutting coachwork (especially the fully-fronted examples built on half-cab chassis) could be thought a little monstrous, but the two Sentinels they handled were treated with taste and style. This is the first of the two, **LNY 307**, originally delivered to Domino Coaches in Barry, South Wales, but pictured with Fenwick, of Old Bolingbrooke, Lincolnshire, its final active owner.

Below: One of the earliest deliveries was to Boyer, of Rothley, who registered their STC4/40 as **GAY 50**, a mark which would surely sell at auction for many thousands of pounds in today's world. The setting is Leicester's St. Margarets bus station and the Midland Red double-decker lurking in the background is symbolic of Boyer's ultimate fate.

39

fledgling preservationist movement and four of the eight vehicles are currently preserved, albeit in varying states of repair.

Browns' delight in their Sentinels was strangely unshared by their Shropshire neighbours at Cooper, Corvedale, and Smiths Eagle, all of whom disposed of their STC4/40s at the first available opportunity. This might suggest that the 'running in' period was more traumatic for 4SRH engines in urban service than for those in long-haul coach employment - Browns' fleet started their lives on 'forces-leave' excursions before being cascaded onto the stage carriage routes.

Next door in Staffordshire, Whieldon's Green Bus took advantage of the Shrewsbury sales and came away with a fleet of four STC6/44s and an STC4/40, later joined by a brand new Burlingham bodied SLC6/30. They had all been sold within three years, replaced by pre-owned double-deckers which offered more capacity but considerably less panache. The biggest beneficiary of this decision was Riviera Services, of Mylor Bridge in Cornwall, which acquired the four low-mileage STC6/44s. One was resold at an early stage, but the other three soldiered on in the Falmouth area until the mid-1960s, giving them a creditable ten years in front-line service on busy routes.

Whieldon's SLC6/30 was sold to Camplejohn Brothers, of Darfield in the West Riding, where it joined two STC6/44s, one bought new, the other a former demonstrator. All three buses passed into Yorkshire Traction ownership in 1961, and the STC6/44s did two years with YTC before heading north for a further three with A.A. Motor Services, Ayr. Once again, a full lifespan, with all of it spent on intensive interurban work.

Routes of a similar nature were operated by Trimdon Motor Services in County Durham, notably a major trunk service from Durham to West Hartlepool. After a long relationship with Dennis and a brief flirtation with Foden, Trimdon paid a visit to the Sentinel emporium in 1954 and came away with ten vehicles ranging from an ex-demonstrator STC4/40 service bus to brand-new SLC6/30 coaches with luxurious A.C.B. Coronation Land Cruiser bodywork. By most accounts they were popular with crews and engineering staff (all ten had direct injection engines) and were later joined by another three second-hand Sentinels. Their end came prematurely when a change in management resulted in a switch to vehicles of lightweight construction, but Durham's loss was the gain of passengers elsewhere.

Trimdon's flagship STC6/44 (OUP 578) ran for a further five years with Baddeley Brothers, of Holmfirth, putting in sterling service in the more strenuous parts of the Pennines, while STC4/40s ended up with operators in Northumberland, Yorkshire, North Wales and Somerset, their OUP registrations giving away their origins wherever they turned up. This must have been particularly galling to travelling north-easterners, forced to endure the Sentinels' Thames Trader replacements.

Coaching fleets

The SLC4/35 coach with Beadle bodywork was not widely admired. Browns took six (with apparent enthusiasm) and Trimdon had three (two of them officially SLC4/27s), but theirs came as part of a lucky-bag in which the main attractions were some succulently cheap service buses. The next largest operator of the type was the Bristol Co-operative Society, trading as Queen of the Road, which took three. BCS had previously shown a penchant for Thornycrofts, so its order for Sentinels was relatively mainstream by comparison. The SLC4/35s were a success and the older two were replaced by SLC6/30s in due course. These machines, one with Plaxton bodywork, the other a Whitson Grand Prix, lasted until 1963 which by coach operator standards is a very long time indeed.

Further north, Benyon, of Atherton in Lancashire, took a new SLC4/35 and followed it with an identical former demonstrator and then a new SLC6/30 with Burlingham Seagull bodywork for a fleet total of three. If all had gone according to plan this total would have been exceeded by Grainger of Smethwick (trading as Eagle Coaches) who took two SLC4/35s and was impressed enough to come back for two of the re-branded SLC4/27s. Before the fleet could grow to four the operator was taken over by another local company (it remained a separate operation until 1960) and the SLC4/27s were cancelled. The existing two

Above: This is Ribble's **CRN 214** in the early 1950s, operating a local service in Carlisle, and still wearing its original livery (with cream rear dome) along with fleet number **2725**. Shortly after this picture was taken it was renumbered as 284 and ten years later would become the only Sentinel to suffer premature withdrawal in the Ribble fleet when it caught fire on the Carlisle-Bowness route.

Below: Readers with long memories may remember that Mid-Wales Motorways vehicles were once painted in an overall green livery. STC4/40 **BEP 864** is seen in Welshpool before its repaint into the later blue and cream livery.

41

vehicles survived until Grainger's eventual absorption into Airflow and then migrated a short distance northwards to Leadbetter (Reddicroft Luxury Coaches), in Sutton Coldfield. The elder of the two was still operational with Collett, of West Bromwich, in 1963: a reasonable lifespan for a coach by anybody's standards.

The six-cylinder coaches fared little better when it came to fleet sales. Blue Cars, a London-based operator of Continental coach tours, took two vehicles, one of them an SLC6/42 originally destined for Argentina but cancelled before delivery, the other one of the SLC6/41s assembled from STC6/44 components. Both were fitted with striking Bellhouse-Hartwell Landmaster bodywork, a choice originally made on the SLC6/41 in deference to Smiths, of Wigan, who had shown an interest in the type. Fortunately, Blue Cars were already familiar with the products of the Westhoughton-based bodybuilder, having received Leyland Royal Tigers with Landmaster bodies and persuaded them to build a second Sentinel body to fit the non-standard dimensions of the SLC6/42 which was 33 feet long and was of left-hand drive. This unusual vehicle, although registered in Britain, was routinely based at Boulogne in France where the authorities were more forgiving of its length, and operated from the French port to Italy, Switzerland and southern Germany. It made occasional visits to London, by special permit on each occasion specifying the precise route to be taken from Dover. Blue Cars passing to the BET Group put paid to prospects of any future orders from the company.

More promising was the interest shown by the Wallace Arnold conglomerate, which dealt in Sentinels through its Wilks and Meade subsidiary. The original demonstrator (Seagull bodied SLC6/30 SUG 19) was rapidly sold to Metcalfe, of Keighley, and replaced by similar machine UUB 931. After a few initial successes orders for SLC6/30s dried up and the second vehicle was transferred to the main Wallace Arnold touring fleet. Despite its unique chassis it remained in stock until 1962 and then saw service with two further operators. It certainly paid for itself many times over.

In the south London area, Sentinel's distributor was Wiggs, a company which also ran a private-hire and excursion business under the name Grey Coaches. Their greatest success was the sale of two SLC6/30s with Duple Elizabethan bodywork to neighbouring operator Lewis, of Greenwich, in 1954. Shortly after this Wiggs was acquired by the Banfield Group, the Sentinel dealership was abandoned, and a Duple-bodied SLC6/30, already at Hendon in final assembly, which had originally been intended for the Grey Coaches fleet was cancelled. Duple paid a visit to Lewis, of Greenwich, who thus increased their stock to three. They were retained until 1963/4 and found further owners upon retirement, in fact the third machine is now preserved after many years as a stock-car transporter.

Some authoritative sources say that Schofield, of Marsden (near Huddersfield in the West Riding of Yorkshire), acquired their Sentinels by way of the Wallace Arnold dealership, but this remains unconfirmed; it does seem logical, particularly given the operator's choice of Burlingham bodywork which was Wallace Arnold's 'default' option. Whatever the source, four were acquired in early 1955, which represented more than half of the small operator's fleet. They apparently performed well and all four passed to Smith when the business (including the Marsden garage) changed hands in April 1958. Three years later the majority of them changed hands for a second time when the business was acquired by Hanson, of Huddersfield. Several photographs confirm their use on the Blackpool express service, but as far as is known they were never used on Hanson's stage carriage routes nor on the Yelloway feeder service which ran in parallel with the Huddersfield-Oldham schedule. Although one was sold almost immediately by its new owner (to see service elsewhere), the remaining two lasted until 1964/5. Curiously, they were never allocated Hanson fleet numbers despite their extended stay, and retained their previous operator's pseudo-Ribble livery throughout.

Sentinel twilight

The four-cylinder engine which powered the STC4/40 and the SLC4/35 was never known for its love of hills and while an agonisingly slow fully-loaded ascent of a hill might be

Above: Davies, of Blackburn, bought two SLC4/35s for a contract service between Blackburn Cathedral and Stoneyhurst, the Catholic seminary near Clitheroe. This is **CCB 584**, the first of the pair. When not needed by Davies they operated on hire to Holmes, of Catterall, complete with that operator's "eyebrow" sign in place of the Davies one shown.

Below: Browns, of Donnington Wood, were justly famous for their fleet of Sentinels, which progressed from operating military leave services to maintaining local bus services around Telford New Town. This is SLC4/35 **HAW 373**, now preserved, at the Donnington terminus of the Rota route.

deemed acceptable to the stage-carriage passengers of Henry Hulley, or Mid-Wales Motorways, who had little alternative except to walk, it rapidly became unfashionable among those renting a private-hire coach where choice was legion.

The tendency for SLC4/35s to gravitate to flatter areas in later life can be illustrated by a couple of examples. NLG 176 (SLC4/35/29, despite the maker's plate), a standard Beadle-bodied example, started life as a distributor's demonstrator with North Cheshire Motors of Stockton Heath, Cheshire, and then ran briefly in service with local coach operator Pitt of Warrington before returning to N.C.M. and being resold to Benyon, of Atherton (later of Tyldesley), along with a factory-fresh example. By 1958 it had moved to Plant, of Rishton, that company having already acquired the two SLC4/35s of Davies, of Blackburn, along with some contract work. Those familiar with the Lancashire terrain will realise that a vehicle operating from either Atherton or Rishton is bound to encounter some impressive gradients, and after disposal by Plant NLG 176 ended its life in easier territory, travelling the gentle swell of the Suffolk countryside in service with Harry Claireaux at Partridge and Son.

Our second example, LNY 307, was one of the two SLC4/35s modified to receive 35-seat bodywork by Gurney Nutting, and was delivered to Domino Coaches of Barry, Glamorgan, in the summer of 1951. Seven years later it was sold and next operated for Dawlish Coaches, in the Devonshire resort of that name. As will be obvious, both Glamorganshire and Devonshire contain many strenuous hills, so the Sentinel duly progressed to a retirement home in flatter terrain, with Fenwick, of Old Bolingbroke, Lincolnshire. At around the same time Fenwick's neighbours, Milson of Coningsby and Grayscroft of Mablethorpe, were also operating Sentinels. In 1963 the vehicle was on the move again, this time within Lincolnshire to arrive at the premises of Smith, Corby Glen. Smith had briefly operated two former Bristol Co-op SLC4/35s in the mid-fifties, no doubt influenced by the Sentinels of Simmons (Reliance Coaches), which operated the stage carriage route from Grantham to Corby Glen, but the new arrival failed to enter service and was subsequently sold to Don Everall, the Wolverhampton dealer. It was then cannibalised of all reusable parts and became increasingly derelict (still wearing Fenwick titles) until being scrapped in 1966. Every Sentinel has its own story to tell, and the bare bones of these tales are encapsulated in the individual vehicle histories which follow.

INDIVIDUAL VEHICLE HISTORIES

The handful of public service vehicles produced by Sentinel in the period up to the Second World War were given construction numbers in the general sequence used for steam waggons with the exception of the Sentinel-HSG which was derived from a Gilford CF176 petrol-powered chassis. The first confirmed PSV (of a kind), the Newcastle Corporation dual-purpose tramway feeder and dung lorry, was based on a stock Standard Sentinel vehicle but its construction number has proven elusive. It carried the registration AW 3918, a Shropshire allocation, which might indicate that it operated on hire from the manufacturer for the duration of the experiment.

This initial vehicle was followed a few years later by the four Super Sentinels. Construction number 5102 was completed in March 1924 and fitted with a 32-seat rear-entrance body by E. and H. Hora, of Peckham. It ran at first on trade-plates and was substantially modified before registration as NT 4950 in 1925. The model failed to find a single UK market customer and the demonstrator was later used by the company's social club as a private runabout. By 1928 it had become a lorry. Similar chassis were despatched to Sentinel's major overseas distributors in the hope of export orders but these fared no better and little is known of their fate after leaving Shrewsbury. For the record they were factory numbers 6147 (exported to the Skoda Works in Czechoslovakia in 1925), 6290 (sent to Griffin Engineering of South Africa, also in 1925), and 6954 (shipped to William Jacks and Company of India in 1927). Reports (or photographic evidence) of the Indian or South African vehicles after export seem to be non-existent, suggesting that they might have ended up in goods configuration despite the original intent. There were certainly

Above: Grainger, of Smethwick (Eagle Coaches), also favoured Sentinels and took delivery of these two SLC4/35s, **RHA 729** and **PHA 928**. Two further vehicles (SLC4/27s) were ordered but never delivered because of a change of ownership.

Below: Portuguese export model **BL-18-52** (SLC6/42/37) was illustrated in an earlier photograph with its original Crespo luxury coach body. This is what it looked like after rebuild with a Leyland engine and being fitted with a new UTIC dual-purpose body.

no repeat orders from overseas for any chassis modified for PSV use.

The solitary example of the Sentinel-HSG, AUX 296, was exhibited at the 1938 Scottish Commercial Motor Show, presumably to capitalise on the work put in by its Gilford-HSG predecessor, which had served with Highland Transport. Despite this existing proof of use in public service, it failed to attract any orders. The vehicle carried construction number H1502 in imitation of the Gilford-HSG machine (registration ST 9465), which had been allocated H1501 by HSG before Sentinel's acquisition of the project. AUX 296 was fitted with a 31-seat, rear-entrance body by Cowieson of Glasgow, another indication that Sentinel had high hopes of orders from north of the border. They never came, and a spell of demonstration to operators in South Wales was similarly unsuccessful. In 1942 the demonstrator was sold to Cooper, of Oakengates, and is now preserved.

The first series of construction numbers used for Sentinel's diesel PSVs covered all variants in a single sequence, with the vehicle number preceded by the model designator. This series covers models SB4/40, STC4/40, STC6/44, SLC4/35, SLC6/41 and SLC6/42. In the case of SB4/40 and most SLC4/35 vehicles a JCB number is given in brackets. This is the number allocated by the coachbuilder John C Beadle to the underframe assembly of the vehicle. On all vehicles, any number given in brackets after the bodywork details is that allocated by the bodybuilder. Not all of these are known.

When the range was restructured in the autumn of 1953, and the model suffix changed to reflect nominal length rather than intended seating capacity, a second series of numbers began. This presented the individual vehicle's identity as a single number, with the first figure representing the number of cylinders in the engine, the second and third the nominal length of the vehicle (to the nearest foot), and any subsequent digits the particular machine within the model designation. To give two examples, 4273 was the third SLC4/27 to be produced, while 63025 was the twenty-fifth SLC6/30. The four SLC4/27s had Beadle underframes and their JCB numbers are recorded as for the first series.

Reading from left to right the heading line for each entry contains the Sentinel factory construction number, the model (perversely not always the same as that given in the works number), the JCB underframe number (where applicable), the bodywork manufacturer (and model name, if any), the seating configuration (see below), and the bodybuilder's construction number (when known). The information on seating and entrance layout uses the standard PSV Circle codes where the initial letters indicate a bus (B), coach (C), or dual-purpose vehicle (DP), the figures in the centre the number of passenger seats, and the final letter the entrance/exit location (C = centre, F = front, R = rear, D = dual). The data given beneath each heading is largely self-explanatory with the exception of the abbreviation 'f/n' which is used to avoid repetition of the words 'fleet number'.

First Series

SB4/40/1 Sentinel-Beadle SB (JCB 30) Beadle B40F (C254)
EUJ 792 Sentinel (Shrewsbury) Ltd 6/48, first prototype and demonstrator. Gave rides to potential customers and members of the press at the Commercial Motor Show 10/48. Delivered to Salopia Saloon Coaches Ltd, Whitchurch, 3/49 as f/n 60. Withdrawn from service 9/61 and later used by an unidentified owner in the Shrewsbury area as a mobile shop. Ultimate fate unknown; no reported sightings after 1962.

SB4/40/2 Sentinel-Beadle SB (JCB 29) Beadle B40F (C253)
Second prototype, completed 3/48 and initially operated on trade-plates. Appeared on the Sentinel stand at the Commercial Motor Show 10/48 in Western National livery. Delivered on long-term hire to Western National Omnibus Company Exeter, 2/49 as HOD 57, f/n 2006 and officially purchased by them 5/52. Withdrawn from service 10/58 and sold to North (dealer), Leeds, and then to Coppock (dealer), Sale, before purchase by Sheriff and Son (Star Service), Gainsborough, in 12/58. Present at AMCC (dealer), London E15 by 2/60, and sold to P. & M. Coach Line, Ipswich, 6/60 as f/n 52. Sold to Claireaux (Partridge and

Above: A brace of Ribble STC6/44s, **DRN 349** and **DRN 346**, at Lowther Street bus station in Carlisle. Film enthusiasts may be able to date the picture from the poster for *The Magnificent Seven*, an early 1960s Western.

Below: The Domino Coaches Gurney Nutting-bodied SLC4/35, photographed before delivery. The location is believed to be Tilstock Aerodrome, a few miles north of the Sentinel factory in Shrewsbury.

47

Son), Layham, 9/62 for use as a spares source for that operator's two active Sentinels. Unwanted remainder to Poole Lane Autos (dealer), Highwood, 2/64, and scrapped.

STC4/40/3 Sentinel STC4/40 Sentinel B40F
Delivered to Boyer, Rothley, 3/50, as GAY 50. Withdrawn from service 1/59 and sold to Monty Moreton, Nuneaton, by 3/59. Withdrawn from use 5/60 and noted operating with Foster, Ellesmere Port, by 8/60. Withdrawn 8/61. Sold to Kershaw (County Coaches), Batford, Hertfordshire, 11/61, remaining in service until 11/62. Sold to Plastow, Wheatley (Oxfordshire) 1/63, and used until 9/66. Ultimate fate unknown.

STC4/40/4 Sentinel STC4/40 Sentinel B40F
Registered to Sentinel (Shrewsbury) Ltd 5/50 as GNT 190 and used as a demonstrator and development vehicle. Sold to Whieldon's Green Bus, Rugeley, 4/53 as f/n 46. Resold to Drew and Wren (Castle), Canterbury, 6/57. Withdrawn from service 12/60 and no further reports. Presumed scrapped.

SLC4/35/5 Sentinel SLC4/35 (JCB 117) Beadle C35C (C310)
Registered to Sentinel (Shrewsbury) Ltd 5/50 as GNT 188. Coach demonstrator. Noted in use with Davies of Blackburn 7/50 - 8/50 and with Isaac (Domino Coaches), Barry, during 1951. Sold to Fielding (Empress Coaches), Bristol, 6/52. Resold to Chard and District (a subsidiary of Wessex Motorways, Bristol) 5/58. Withdrawn from service 6/59 and no further sightings.

SB4/40/6 Sentinel-Beadle SB (JCB 83) Beadle B40F (C257)
Completed 1/49 and initially operated on tradeplates. Delivered to Ribble Motor Services, Preston, 5/49 as CRN 211, f/n 2722 (changed to 278 in 12/50). Sold to Cowley (dealer), Salford, 8/63. Resold to Toogood, Kenilworth, 10/64 for use as a mobile shop. Last reported 9/65.

STC4/40/7 Sentinel STC4/40 Sentinel B40F
Delivered to Ribble Motor Services, Preston, 2/50 as CRN 212, f/n 2723 (changed to 279 by 5/52). Sold to Cowley (dealer), Salford, 8/63. Remained unsold and scrapped 5/65.

STC4/40/8 Sentinel STC4/40 Sentinel B40F
Delivered to Ribble Motor Services, Preston, 5/50 as CRN 213, f/n 2724 (280 in 1952). Sold to Cowley (dealer), Salford, 8/63. Remained unsold and scrapped.

STC4/40/9 Sentinel STC4/40 Sentinel B40F
Delivered to Ribble Motor Services, Preston, 5/50 as CRN 214, f/n 2725 (281 in 1952). Engine fire in service at Bowness-on-Solway 17/10/62 and remains scrapped locally in 11/62.

STC4/40/10 Sentinel STC4/40 Sentinel B40F
Delivered to Ribble Motor Services, Preston, 5/50 as CRN 215, f/n 2726 (282 in 1952). Sold to Cowley (dealer), Salford, 5/63. Resold to J C Shone, Widnes, 2/64 for use as a mobile shop. Withdrawn from use 12/64 and believed scrapped.

STC4/40/11 Sentinel STC4/40 Sentinel B40F
Delivered to Ribble Motor Services, Preston, 7/50 as CRN 216, f/n 2727 (283 by 5/53). Sold to Cowley (dealer), Salford, 4/63. Sold to Norwest Construction, Liverpool, 6/64 and subsequently used as a site hut in the Sheffield area. Fate unknown, but last sighted in poor condition and presumed scrapped.

STC4/40/12 Sentinel STC4/40 Sentinel B40F
Delivered to Dickson, Dundee, 4/50 as AYJ 822, f/n 3. Withdrawn by 12/52 and next reported with Mundy (Silver Queen), Camborne, 3/53. Withdrawn by them in 12/56 and sold to Pooley (Pamela Coaches), Long Sutton, 6/57. Withdrawn from use 6/63 and scrapped 11/66.

SLC4/35/13 Sentinel SLC4/35 (JCB 120) Beadle C35C (C313)
Supplied via North Cheshire Motors (dealer) to Davies, Blackburn, 7/50 as CCB 673. Operated by Davies on a schools contract during termtime and on hire to Holmes, of Catterall, complete with their fleetnames, during summer holidays in 1950-2 seasons and possibly later. Sold to Plant, Rishton, 5/57. Operating with Rafferty, Coatbridge, by 11/60. Fate unknown.

STC4/40/14 Sentinel STC4/40 Sentinel B40F
Delivered to Cooper, Oakengates, 8/50 as GNT

Above: Among the many small Welsh independents tempted by Sentinels was Pritchard, of Narberth, who took delivery of this Beadle-bodied SLC4/35, **NDE 689**. The location is alongside the Swansea factory of EKCO, who once manufactured radios, and the shot is dated September 1952.

Below: The Bristol Co-operative Society, trading as *Queen of the Road* was an enthusiastic purchaser of Sentinels throughout the brief production period. This is Beadle-bodied SLC4/35 **NHY 637** in the first livery of red and cream with fawn trim, seen at Marlborough in the early 1950s.

961. Returned to Sentinel 5/52 and resold to Delaine Coaches, Bourne, 6/52 as f/n 36. Sold to Whippet, Hilton 5/58. Sold to Mid-Wales Motorways, Newtown, 3/60. Destroyed in garage fire 19/7/69.

STC4/40/15 Sentinel STC4/40 Sentinel B40F
Delivered to Wigmore, Dinnington, 4/50 as JWW 316. Withdrawn 12/53 and next reported with Enterprise, Otterhampton, Somerset, 3/54. Withdrawn by them 1/57 and sold to Talbott (Barry's Coaches), Moreton-in-the-Marsh, 7/57. Withdrawn from use 2/59 and sold to Barnard & Barnard (dealer), London SE26. Resold to Horlock, Northfleet, 3/59 but then returned to dealer in 9/59. Next reported with Claireaux (Partridge and Son), Layham, 1/60. Withdrawn from service 2/62, and sold to Sacker (scrap dealer), Ipswich, in 1963.

STC4/40/16 Sentinel STC4/40 Sentinel B40F
Delivered to Mid-Wales Motorways 4/50 as BEP 864 (a report of the vehicle being completed in 4/49 is believed to be an error). Destroyed by fire at the Newtown garage on 19/7/69 after more than 19 years in service with its original operator.

STC4/40/17 Sentinel STC4/40 Sentinel B40F
Originally intended as European demonstrator (left hand drive) for Ramshorst, Amsterdam, but never delivered as such and eventually registered to Sentinel (Shrewsbury) in 1952 as JUX 270. Used as a UK demonstrator before sale to Trimdon Motor Services 12/53 as f/n 24. Reregistered as OUP 581 upon repaint into fleet livery 5/54. Sold to Hughes (dealer), Bradford, 10/60, and then to Hallen Coaches, Bristol, 11/60. Returned to Hughes in 1/61 after fire damage, repaired, and sold to Hoyle (contractor), Halifax, 8/61. Withdrawn from use 7/64 and scrapped.

STC4/40/18 Sentinel STC4/40 Sentinel B40F
Delivered to Ramshorst (dealer), Amsterdam, in early 1952 for display and demonstrations at the RAI Show. Engine mountings failed whilst on demonstration rides and returned to Sentinel. Registered JUJ 264 and sold (engineless) to Brown, Donnington Wood, 3/53 who fitted it with a spare unit acquired with their SLC4/35 fleet. Withdrawn from use in 5/71 and sold to Greenhous (dealer), Hereford, but remained at Donnington Wood and scrapped on site later in 1971.

SLC4/35/19 Sentinel SLC4/35 (JCB 118) Beadle C35C (C311)
Delivered via North Cheshire Motors to Davies, Blackburn, 6/50, as CCB 584. Operated on hire to Holmes, Catterall, in summer months of 1950-2 (and possibly later) with Holmes fleetnames in eyebrow blinds. Sold to Plant, Rishton, 5/57 and last reported with them in late 1960. Fate unknown.

STC4/40/20 Sentinel STC4/40 Sentinel B40F
Registered to Sentinel (Shrewsbury) 7/50 as GNT 587 and used as a demonstrator. Sold in as seen condition (still fitted with original indirect injection engine) to Richardson (Majestic Motors), Thorne, 5/52. Operator acquired by Morgan (Blue Line), Armthorpe, in 12/53 and vehicle withdrawn from use by Morgan in 3/55. Placed in open storage at Stainforth premises of associated company Store (Reliance) and noted still present but derelict in 4/62. Remains sold to Smith (dealer), Bentley, 4/64 and scrapped on site.

SLC4/35/21 Sentinel SLC4/35 (JCB 121) Beadle C35C (C314)
Delivered to Lloyd-Jones Brothers, Pontrhydygroes, 6/51, as BEJ 190. Withdrawn from use in 2/57 and next reported with Clark (Castle Coaches), North Shields, 12/58. Sold to Patterson, Bradnell, Northumberland, 3/59. Sold to Jopling, Birtley, County Durham 7/60. Sold to Moseley (dealer), Loughborough, 6/61. Believed scrapped.

SLC4/35/22 Sentinel SLC4/35 (JCB 123) Beadle C35C (C315)
Delivered to Brown, Donnington Wood, 5/51, as HAW 373. Converted to DP41F lay-out in 1966 with bus seats, front entrance, and equipment for one-man-operation. Sold to Wheatley, Kenilworth, 12/71 for preservation, and reconverted to original centre-entrance configuration. Still owned and stored in Herefordshire.

SLC4/35/23 Sentinel SLC4/35 (JCB 124) Beadle C35C (C316)

Above: Bristol Co-op's Sentinels were later repainted into this much less exciting colour scheme. **PAE 596** remained at Fishponds long after the other two SLC4/35s had departed, keeping company with their replacement SLC6/30s until the early 1960s.

Below: Wiggs, of London SE15, were a Sentinel dealership and also operated a private-hire and excursion business trading as Grey Coaches. Their Plaxton Venturer-bodied SLC4/35, **MYR 500**, served both as a demonstrator and as a working coach. The Venturer body was offered in either 7ft 6ins or 8ft widths, and this is the narrower version flanked by eight-footers from Duple and ECW.

Incorrectly plated as STC4/40/23. Registered to Sentinel (Shrewsbury) 8/51 as HNT 101 and used as a demonstrator. Sold to Brown, Donnington Wood, 3/53. Converted to DP37C configuration by 1/68 (bus seats) and then to DP41F (omo) between 2/69 and 11/69. Withdrawn from service 11/11/73 and sold to Wheatley (preservationist), Kenilworth, 12/73. Dismantled at Donnington Wood for use as spares.

STC4/40/24 Sentinel STC4/40 Sentinel B40F
Delivered to Edwards Brothers Motors, Crymmych, 9/51, as NDE 799. Business sold to Messrs Rees and Phillips in 1957, trading as Midway Motors. Withdrawn from use 10/57, and next noted with Willis, Bodmin, 3/58. Withdrawn by them in 6/60 and almost certainly the vehicle seen in use as a horticultural shed near St Mabyn, Cornwall, as late as 1964 (although this is unconfirmed by a plate-check), Ultimate fate unknown, but presumed scrapped locally.

STC4/40/25 Sentinel STC4/40 Sentinel B40F
Delivered to Corvedale Motors, Ludlow, 3/51, as GUX 524, f/n 30. Sold to Chapple, Raglan, 2/54. Returned to Corvedale in 9/57 and allocated f/n 24. Sold to Mid-Wales Motorways, Newtown, 10/58. Withdrawn from service 4/70 and scrapped.

SLC4/35/26 Sentinel SLC4/35 (JCB 125) Beadle C35C (C317)
Delivered to Warners Motors, Tewkesbury, 6/51, as KDG 853. Sold to Sargeant Brothers, Kington, 5/59. Sold to Darlow, Nottingham, 7/60. Sold to Bonser & Gospel, Bulwell 2/61, and then ownership transferred to Gospel (as sole proprietor), Bulwell, 12/62. Out of use by 12/63 and next reported with Sergent, Wrinehill, 4/64. One report suggests that Sergent withdrew it as early as 8/64, but next reported with Williams, Gloucester, 9/65. Withdrawn from service 2/66 and later scrapped.

STC4/40/27 Sentinel STC4/40 Sentinel B40F
Delivered to Connor & Graham, Easington, 3/51, as JWF 176. Sold to Jones (Caelloi Motors), Pwllheli, 9/60. Gone by 11/64, fate unknown.

SLC4/35/28 Sentinel SLC4/35 (JCB 126) Beadle C35C (C318)
Exhibited at Commercial Motor Show 10/50 in livery of Wigmore, Dinnington, but never owned by them. Delivered to Grainger (Eagle Coaches), Smethwick, 7/51 as PHA 928. Sold to Leadbetter (Reddicroft Luxury Coaches), Sutton Coldfield, 9/60. Sold to Trott, Birmingham 4/63, but not used and resold the same month to Collett, West Bromwich. Withdrawn from use 6/63 and scrapped after several months in open storage.

SLC4/35/29 Sentinel SLC4/35 (JCB 119) Beadle C35C (C312)
Vehicle identity plate carried STC4/40/29 in error. Registered to North Cheshire Motors (distributor), Stockton Heath, 9/50 as NLG 176. Sold to Pitt, Warrington, 9/50. Returned to North Cheshire Motors 2/51. Sold to Benyon, Atherton, 6/51. Sold to Plant, Rishton, in 1957, withdrawn by them in 7/60. Sold to Claireaux (Partridge and Son) 5/61. Withdrawn from use in 1964 and later scrapped by Poole Lane Autos (dealer), Highwood.

STC4/40/30 Sentinel STC4/40 Sentinel B40F
Registered to Sentinel (Shrewsbury), 11/50, as GUJ 608, and used as a demonstrator. Sold to Leader (Maryland Luxury Coaches), London E15, 1/52. Sold to Warners Motors, Tewkesbury, 12/55. Sold to Brown, Donnington Wood, 1/59. Withdrawn from use 7/71. Sold to Gray (preservationist), Moseley, 2/72 and currently displayed at Aston Manor Transport Museum.

STC4/40/31 Sentinel STC4/40 Sentinel B40F
Registered to Sentinel (Shrewsbury) 10/50 as GUJ 457. Originally intended for Cooper, Oakengates, and painted in their livery, but probably not delivered (one report states that it was used in service by Cooper for one week at Xmas 1950, but this could have been on hire from the manufacturers). Used as a demonstrator, still in Cooper livery, throughout 1951, then sold as seen to Richardson (Majestic Motors), Thorne, 3/52, complete with indirect injection engine. Business acquired by Morgan (Blue Line), Armthorpe, 12/53. Withdrawn from use 12/58 and placed in open storage at Stainforth depot of associated company Store

Above: Plaxton completed this 8ft-wide vehicle in the winter of 1952 and then placed it into storage at Scarborough until March 1954. Its eventual purchaser (presumably at a steeply discounted price) was Seagull Coaches, Great Yarmouth, who registered it as **EX 8344**. Great Yarmouth, along with Bootle in Lancashire, was one of the last English authorities to issue marks with a two-letter prefix.

Below: Grainger's Beadle-bodied SLC4/35 **RHA 729** at an unknown industrial location somewhere in the West Midlands. After withdrawal by Grainger in 1960 the vehicle served for a further two years with Leadbetter of Sutton Coldfield.

(Reliance). Still there, in derelict condition, 4/67, but remains sold to Winter (dealer), Newark, 1/71, and scrapped on site at Stainforth.

STC4/40/32 Sentinel STC4/40 Sentinel B40F
Delivered to Potter (Tor Bus), Haytor, 7/50, as LOD 974. Sold to Venner, Witheridge, 12/56. Sold to Heard, Hartland, 5/57. Withdrawn from use 10/58 and sold to Arlington (dealer), London SW1 2/59. Resold to the Civil Defence Establishment at the Porton Down germ warfare base in Wiltshire 3/59. Initially used as a photographic training unit and later as a static mess hut within the top secret installation. Sold at auction 8/80 and purchased by Colin Shears (preservationist), Winkleigh. Resold in 4/81 to a syndicate of nine owners and external restoration now complete. Roadworthy and based in Devonshire.

SLC4/35/33 Sentinel SLC4/35 (JCB 127) Beadle C35C (C319)
Delivered to Brown, Donnington Wood, 5/51, as HAW 374. Converted to DP37C lay-out (bus seats) 4/67. Withdrawn from use 11/69 and placed in open storage at the depot. Broken up for scrap 6/72 after some body parts (including the central entrance bay and door components) were removed to assist in the restoration of sister vehicle HAW 373 (SLC4/35/22).

SLC6/42/34 Sentinel SLC6/42 Park Royal B42D (B34513)
Exhibited at Commercial Motor Show, 10/50, before export to Viacao Nacional, Rio de Janeiro, Brazil. Five more similar vehicles were originally ordered (and allocated body numbers by Park Royal) but never delivered. Brazilian registration and fate unknown.

SLC6/42/35 Sentinel SLC6/42 Gaya Perez ????
Intended as second vehicle of Brazilian order, but exported to Gaya Perez, Montevideo, Uruguay during 1952. This company built bus bodywork, but no further details have emerged concerning configuration or subsequent operators, and some authorities claim that no Sentinel buses have ever operated in Uruguay while others refer obliquely to this vehicle without specific information. Fate unknown !

SLC6/42/36 Sentinel SLC6/42 ???? ????
Also reported as model SOT6/42 - see Note 1. Originally intended for Brazil, then earmarked for Uruguay, but actually delivered to Viacao da Beira, Pampilhosa da Serra, Portugal, 9/52, as GC-18-68. Original bodywork details unknown. Sold to A P Marques, Pedrogao Grande, 1/60. Rebuilt during 1962 with a Leyland O.600 engine, pneumocyclic gearbox, and new UTIC B43D body. Sold to Empresa da Transportes Rodoviaria Nacional, Zezere, 3/63 as f/n 3062. Last reported sighting in 9/68 - fate unknown.

SLC6/42/37 Sentinel SLC6/42 P. & F. Crespo C30D
Also reported as model SOT6/42 - see Note 1. Originally for Brazil, then Uruguay, then delivered to Isadore Duarte, Povoa da Galega, Portugal, 9/52 as BL-18-52, f/n 25. Rebuilt in 1965 with a Leyland O.600 engine, pneumocyclic gearbox, and a new UTIC DP43D body. This is almost certainly the vehicle reported operating local services on the island of Santa Maria (Azores) in 5/67, but no details have come to light concerning its operator there. Fate unknown.

STC4/40/38 Sentinel STC4/40 Sentinel B40F
Delivered to Roberts (Pioneer), Newport, Pembrokeshire, 7/51, as NDE 620. Sold to Martin, Weaverham, 6/59. Sold to Simpson, Cardenden 11/60, then to Don Everall (dealer), Wolverhampton, 6/61. Sold to Mitchell, Wednesbury, 10/61 for use as a mobile shop. Returned to Everall 1/62 and believed scrapped after leaving the site in 2/62.

STC6/44/39 Sentinel STC6/44 Sentinel B44F
Delivered to Ribble Motor Services, Preston, 2/51 as DRN 341, f/n 284. Sold to Cowley (dealer), Salford, 8/63. Resold to Parham (contractor), Gillingham, 9/63. Fate unknown.

STC6/44/40 Sentinel STC6/44 Sentinel B44F
Delivered to Ribble Motor Services, Preston, 2/51 as DRN 342, f/n 285. Sold to Cowley (dealer), Salford, 8/63. Still owned by Cowley in 4/65 and later scrapped.

STC6/44/41 Sentinel STC6/44 Sentinel B44F
Delivered to Ribble Motor Services, Preston,

Above: Many of the Trimdon Motor Services coaches carried the Bluebird fleet-name but here we see Beadle-bodied SLC4/35 **PPT 212** in full TMS livery. After Trimdon's decision to sell its Sentinels, the vehicle saw further use in Scotland and the Republic of Ireland.

Below: One of four STC4/E chassis delivered to importer George Lee, of Singapore, this vehicle was fitted with central-entrance bodywork by an unknown local manufacturer and then sold to the Tay Koh Yat bus company as **SH 190**. The meaning of the letter in the top corner of the radiator grille remains obscure.

2/51 as DRN 343, f/n 286. Sold to Cowley (dealer), Salford, 8/63. Resold to Parham (contractor), Gillingham, 9/63 but not used and kept as a source of spares for STC6/44/39. Remainder scrapped.

STC6/44/42 Sentinel STC6/44 Sentinel B44F
Delivered to Ribble Motor Services, Preston, 2/51 as DRN 344, f/n 287. Sold to Cowley (dealer), Salford, 8/63. Sold to Sproat (Cedar Coaches), Bedford, 8/63. Next reported in use as a mobile cafe by an unknown owner in the Nottingham area 9/65 and sometimes to be found parked outside Broad Marsh bus station in that city. Later passed to Bishton (dealer), Dunkirk, Notts, and scrapped.

STC6/44/43 Sentinel STC6/44 Sentinel B44F
Delivered to Ribble Motor Services, Preston, 2/51 as DRN 345, f/n 288. Sold to Cowley (dealer), Salford, 8/63. Resold to Millburn Motors (dealer), Preston, 3/64. Sold to Parkinson (contractor), Blackpool, 10/64. Withdrawn from use 6/68 and scrapped 11/68.

STC6/44/44 Sentinel STC6/44 Sentinel B44F
Delivered to Ribble Motor Services, Preston, 2/51 as DRN 346, f/n 289. Sold to Cowley (dealer), Salford, 8/63. Sold to Ashley (contractor), Mansfield Woodhouse, 2/64. Returned to Cowley 2/67 and sold for scrap 11/68.

STC6/44/45 Sentinel STC6/44 Sentinel B44F
Delivered to Ribble Motor Services, Preston, 2/51 as DRN 347, f/n 290. Sold to Cowley (dealer), Salford, 8/63. Sold to Rossmore Bus Company, Sandbanks, 11/63. Withdrawn from use 2/64, reported derelict at depot 4/66, and later scrapped.

STC6/44/46 Sentinel STC6/44 Sentinel B44F
Delivered to Ribble Motor Services, Preston, 3/51 as DRN 348, f/n 291. Sold to Cowley (dealer), Salford, 8/63. Sold to Clynnog & Trevor Motor Co., Trevor, 9/63. Reportedly only used in service for a matter of weeks, but not officially withdrawn until 6/64. Placed in open storage and in use as a storage shed by 1966. Later scrapped.

STC6/44/47 Sentinel STC6/44 Sentinel B44F
Delivered to Ribble Motor Services, Preston, 3/51 as DRN 349, f/n 292. Sold to Cowley (dealer), Salford, 8/63. Sold to Edwards, Llangeinor, 10/63. Withdrawn from use 2/66 and sold for scrap to a local dealer.

STC6/44/48 Sentinel STC6/44 Sentinel B44F
Delivered to Ribble Motor Services, Preston, 3/51 as DRN 350, f/n 293. Sold to Cowley (dealer), Salford, 8/63. Sold to Rodgers (Station Taxis), Redcar, 8/63. Withdrawn from use 7/64 and returned to Cowley 8/65 for scrap.

STC6/44/49 Sentinel STC6/44 Sentinel B44F
Delivered to Ribble Motor Services, Preston, 3/51 as DRN 351, f/n 294. Sold to Cowley (dealer), Salford, 8/63. Sold to Rossmore Bus Company, Sandbanks, 11/63 for use as spares for STC6/44/45, but believed never delivered to Dorset and scrapped by Cowley.

STC6/44/50 Sentinel STC6/44 Sentinel B44F
Delivered to Ribble Motor Services, Preston, 4/51 as DRN 352, f/n 295. Sold to Cowley (dealer), Salford, 8/63. Sold to Croston (contractor), Lowton 5/64 but continued to be based at Cowley's Pennington yard (Lowton is the adjacent suburb of Leigh) until at least 5/65 while in regular use. Fate unknown.

STC6/44/51 Sentinel STC6/44 Sentinel B44F
Delivered to Ribble Motor Services, Preston, 5/51 as DRN 353, f/n 296. Sold to Cowley (dealer), Salford, 8/63. Licenced by Cowley 1/64 until 4/64 and noted during this period operating for Ross Insulation, Formby. Returned to dealer stock and later scrapped.

STC6/44/52 Sentinel STC6/44 Sentinel B44F
Delivered to Ribble Motor Services, Preston, 5/51 as DRN 354, f/n 297. Sold to Cowley (dealer), Salford, 8/63. Still owned 4/65 and later scrapped.

SLC4/35/53 Sentinel SLC4/35 (JCB 128) Beadle C35C (C320)
Delivered to Bristol Co-operative Society (Queen of the Road), Fishponds, Bristol, 3/51 as NHY 465, f/n 39. Withdrawn from service 7/54 and sold to Smith, Groby, Leicestershire. Resold within weeks to Mellor, Littlethorpe (also Leicestershire), and then to Jollands,

Above: **JNT 763** was the last STC6/44 allocated as a demonstrator and is seen here operating in County Durham for Trimdon Motor Services. Trimdon bought the vehicle shortly afterwards and reregistered it as OUP 578 at repaint into fleet livery. It had a second career with Baddeley Brothers, of Holmfirth in Yorkshire, from 1960 until 1965, after which it was scrapped.

Below: A Sentinel advertisement image of the Blue Cars Bellhouse-Hartwell-bodied SLC6/41 **NLR 850**. The vehicle was equipped with 32 luxurious reclining seats and a food-servery area, which is visible at the nearside rear-end.

Blaby, in 9/58. Withdrawn by them in 11/60 and then next noted with Turner Brothers, Pegswood, Northumberland, from 5/61- 8/61. Operating with Caterer (Icknield Coaches), Tring, Hertfordshire by 10/62 and then sold to Woolley & English (Dartmoor Bus Company), Haccombe, Devonshire. 9/63. Withdrawn from use 5/64 and scrapped.

SLC4/35/54 Sentinel SLC4/35 (JCB 129) Beadle C35C (C321)
Delivered to Brown, Donnington Wood, 5/51, as HAW 302. Converted to DP41F (bus seats, omo) by 11/68. Withdrawn from service 25/11/73. Sold to Wheatley (preservationist), Kenilworth, 12/73. Kept as a spares source but still basically intact at a private location in Herefordshire.

SLC4/35/55 Sentinel SLC4/35 Gurney Nutting C35C (1164)
Delivered to Isaac (Domino Coaches), Barry, 8/51 as LNY 307. Business transferred to Adams, Barry, 6/56, still operating as Domino. Sold to Tomlinson (Dawlish Coaches), Dawlish, 5/58. Sold to Hughes (dealer), Bradford, 10/59, and then to Fenwick, Old Bolingbroke (Lincs) 11/59. Sold to Smith, Corby Glen (Lincs) 7/63 but never repainted and probably never used. Sold to Don Everall (dealer), Wolverhampton, 5/64. Remained unsold and passed to Gammell (scrap merchant), Bloxwich, 2/66.

SLC4/35/56 Sentinel SLC4/35 (JCB 130) Beadle C35C (C322)
Delivered via North Cheshire Motors (distributor), Stockton Heath, to Benyon, Atherton, 6/51 as NTB 955 (reported as f/n 11 by one correspondent). Sold to Stokes (Willows Coaches), Liverpool, 5/56. Sold to Pooley (Pamela Coaches) of Long Sutton in 3/58, but never entered service and was used to provide spares for STC4/40/12. Last reported 7/63.

SLC4/35/57 Sentinel SLC4/35 (JCB 133) Beadle C35C (C325)
Completed 11/50 and registration HAW 588 allegedly reserved by Sentinel but no official confirmation of this can be found. Delivered to Pritchard, Narberth (Pembrokeshire) 9/51, as NDE 689. Sold to Edwards Brothers Motors, Crymmych 6/53. Business transferred to Messrs Rees & Phillips (Midway Motors) in 1957. Sold to Humphries & Thomas, Haverfordwest, 3/58 and then resold to Gravell, Kidwelly 5/58 and to Howells of Burry Port by 11/58. Sold to O'Connor & Davies (contractor), Llanelli, 7/65 and presumed scrapped shortly thereafter. Tax record voided in 1972.

SLC4/35/58 Sentinel SLC4/35 (JCB 131) Beadle C35C (C323)
Delivered to Bristol Co-operative Society (Queen of the Road), Fishponds, Bristol, 5/51 as NHY 637, f/n 40. Sold to Smith, Corby Glen (Lincs) 8/53 but 'wrecked' (no details found) 7/54 and remains sold to Don Everall (dealer), Wolverhampton. Burned on site during 1955.

SLC4/35/59 Sentinel SLC4/35 (JCB 132) Beadle C35C (C324)
Delivered to Brown, Donnington Wood, 5/51, as HAW 303. Converted to DP41F lay-out (bus seats, omo) 4/65. Withdrawn from service 11/70 and sold to Greenhous (dealer), Hereford. Remained at Donnington Wood and broken up there in 6/72.

SLC4/35/60 Sentinel SLC4/35 (JCB 134) Beadle C35C (C326)
Delivered to Bristol Co-operative Society (Queen of the Road), Fishponds, Bristol, 6/52, as PAE 596, f/n 41. Sold to Bristol-Siddeley Engines, Filton, 8/62 for use by the works social club. Sold to Bugler Coaches, Bristol, 9/64. Sold to Don Everall (dealer), Wolverhampton, 5/65 and then resold to John, Tonypandy, 6/65. Withdrawn from use 11/66, and no further sightings.

SLC4/35/61 Sentinel SLC4/35 Plaxton Venturer C37C (1881)
Built to 7ft 6ins width and 29ft 2ins length. Delivered to Wiggs (Grey Coaches), London SE15 in 7/52 as MYR 500. Used both in service and as a demonstrator. Sold to Spiers, Henley-on-Thames, 4/54. Withdrawn from service in early 1965 and sold in roadworthy condition for further use, but no further reports.

SLC4/35/62 Sentinel SLC4/35 Plaxton Venturer C37C (1879)

Above: The other Blue Cars Sentinel/Bellhouse-Hartwell was the famous SLC6/42 which rarely graced British soil, **MYV 637**. Originally ordered by the Argentinian operator Drake, the chassis never reached South America but did roam far and wide across continental Europe while in service with Blue Cars. The interior was largely identical to that of NLR 850, but used the extra length to accommodate a toilet compartment as well as a servery and additional luggage space.

Below: The SLC4/27 was marketed in a last-ditch attempt to reduce the stockpiles of Beadle C35C bodywork components (and 4SRH engines). Only four were sold, and this is numerically the first, **NWO 122**. Originally built for Grainger, of Smethwick, it ended up in the fleet of Chapple, of Raglan, and is seen in the depot of this small Monmouthshire operator. The vehicle was later rescued from a scrapyard and is now in storage.

Built to a width of 8ft and a length of 29ft 2ins. Completed by Plaxton 6/52 as a speculative vehicle and placed in store at Scarborough. Sold to Seagull Coaches, Great Yarmouth, 3/54, as EX 8344. Sold to Pegg, Caston, 3/60. Sold to Saunders, Waddesdon (Bucks), 7/62. Sold on in roadworthy condition 2/63, but no further reports.

SLC4/35/63 Sentinel SLC4/35 (JCB 137) Beadle C35C (C328)
Delivered to Brown, Donnington Wood, 7/51, as HNT 49. Converted to DP41F (bus seats, omo) 12/66. Withdrawn from use 12/71 and sold to Farnham (preservationist), Birmingham, 3/72. Resold later in the same year to Cook et al (preservationists), Reading, and placed into storage at Sandtoft. Sold to Wheatley (preservationist), Kenilworth, 1/82. Still owned and currently stored at a private location in Herefordshire.

SLC4/35/64 Sentinel SLC4/35 Gurney Nutting C35C
Delivered to Thomas, North Muskham, 5/52 as NAL 333. Next reported operating with Nesbit, Somerby, 5/60-8/60, and then sold to an unknown operator (or dealer?) in Northamptonshire. Sold to Frost, Weston Coyney (Staffs), by 1962. Operator ceased trading in 1963 but vehicle retained in unlicensed condition until at least 8/65. Gone by the following summer and presumed scrapped.

SLC4/35/65 Sentinel SLC4/35 (JCB 135) Beadle C35C (C327)
Completed 7/51 and stored by Beadle. Delivered to Grainger (Eagle Coaches), Smethwick, 4/52 as RHA 729. Sold to Leadbetter (Reddicroft Luxury Coaches), Sutton Coldfield, 9/60. Withdrawn from use 2/62 and later scrapped by a local dealer.

SLC4/35/66 Sentinel SLC4/35 (JCB 136) Beadle C35C (C329)
Originally booked for Morgan, Corse Lawn, in 1952 but cancelled before delivery. Stored by Beadle until sale to Trimdon Motor Services 6/54 as PPT 212, f/n 5. Sold to Calvert & Skelton, Eston, 7/60, but returned within weeks and resold to Ford, Fairburn, 8/60. Sold to Hughes (dealer), Bradford, 12/60 and then to Blackmore, Glasgow, 5/61. Next sighted in County Cork, Ireland (with no visible sign of ownership) in 1966/7. By 2/68 withdrawn from use and owned by a dealer at Edgeworthstown. Remained there (in increasingly derelict condition) until scrapped in 2002, narrowly evading preservation.

SLC4/35/67 Sentinel SLC4/35 Plaxton Venturer C37C (1880)
Fitted with 8ft wide bodywork to a length of 29ft 2ins. Completed 6/52 and stored until delivery to Horton (Sunbeam Coaches), West Bromwich, 2/53 as HEA 433. Sold to Taylor, Henwick (Worcester), 5/53 as f/n 8. Sold to Jones, High House, 8/58. Sold to Superb Coaches, Birmingham, 10/60 and then resold to Saxton, Heanor, 11/60. Sold to Grayscroft, Mablethorpe, 3/61. Sold to Yeates (dealer), Loughborough, 9/62. Later reported operating as a mobile shop. No further sightings and presumed scrapped.

STC4/40/68 Sentinel STC4/40 Sentinel B40F
Delivered to Corvedale Motors, Ludlow, 5/51, as HAW 180, f/n 29. Sold to Delaine Coaches, Bourne, 9/53, as f/n 38. Sold to Morley, Whittlesey, 11/58. Withdrawn from service 6/63 and believed scrapped by a local dealer.

STC4/40/69 Sentinel STC4/40 Sentinel B40F
Delivered to Moffit, Acomb, 2/51, as ETY 174, f/n 5. Business acquired by Charlton, Newborough, 10/58, and vehicle's fleet number changed to A5. Sold to Reed (Service Coaches), Bebside, 12/60. Sold to Appleby (Terrier Coaches), Choppington, 7/62. Withdrawn from use by 3/63 and later scrapped.

STC4/40/70 Sentinel STC4/40 Sentinel B40F
Delivered to Mid-Wales Motorways, Newtown, 5/51, as CEP 147. Destroyed in garage fire at Newtown 19/7/69 after more than 18 years with its original operator.

STC4/40/71 Sentinel STC4/40 Sentinel B40F
Delivered to Harries (Prendergast Motors), Prendergast, 1/52, as ODE 40. Sold to Trimdon Motor Services 7/58 as f/n 40. Sold to Calvert & Skelton, Eston, 11/59, but returned to

Above: The other SLC4/27 intended for Grainger was sold to Back of Witney (in Oxfordshire) and registered as **HBW 505**. It is seen here at Oxford's Gloucester Green bus station, waiting to operate a South Midland duplicate to Southsea.

Below: Bristol Co-op took two SLC6/30 coaches, one with Whitson Grand Prix bodywork, the other a Plaxton Venturer built to a new design as seen here. Originally registered as RHW 233 in 9/53, delivery of the vehicle was deferred until the start of the new season. Anxious to emphasise the newness of its arrival, Bristol Co-op allowed the RHW registration to lapse and the vehicle became **SHT 468**.

Trimdon 4/60. Sold to Waller, Stockton-on-Tees, 9/60 for conversion into a mobile shop. Believed scrapped by 9/64.

STC4/40/72 Sentinel STC4/40 Sentinel B40F
Delivered to K.W. Services, Daventry, 7/51, as GRP 105, f/n S1. Sold to Gee & Harrison, Whittington (Staffs) 12/57. Sold to Don Everall (dealer), Wolverhampton, 5/61, and then resold to Whittingham (contractor), Wolverhampton, 8/61. Returned to Everalls 9/63 and then sold to Gammell (scrap merchant), Bloxwich, 3/64.

STC4/40/73 Sentinel STC4/40 Sentinel B40F
Completed 10/53 and delivered to Trimdon Motor Services 3/54 as OUP 579, f/n 14. Sold to Oddy (contractor), Stainland, 2/55, and then to Hughes (dealer), Bradford, in 5/56. Sold to Gee & Harrison, Whittington (Staffs), 6/57. Sold to Don Everall (dealer), Wolverhampton, 5/61, then resold to Phillips (Ceiriog Valley Transport), Glyn Ceiriog, 6/61. Returned to Everalls 8/61, and resold to Longstaff, Ravensthorpe, 11/61. Sold to Phillips Coach Company, Shiptonthorpe, 11/65. Withdrawn from use 11/66 and later scrapped.

STC4/40/74 Sentinel STC4/E ???? B37F
Delivered to George Lee (vehicle importer), Singapore, in 1952, and equipped with locally built service-bus bodywork. This vehicle was the first of four and two of the batch (tie-ups unknown) received the registration marks SH 190 and SH 191 with the Tay Koh Yat bus company. As delivered to this operator they were originally of front-entrance configuration but were later converted to dual-door. The other two chassis remain untraced.

STC4/40/75 Sentinel STC4/E
See entry for STC4/40/74.

STC4/40/76 Sentinel STC4/E
See entry for STC4/40/74.

STC4/40/77 Sentinel STC4/40 Sentinel B40F
Delivered to Smith (Smiths Eagle), Trench, 4/51, as HAW 179. Sold to Nickolls, Milford, 9/52. Sold to Sergent, Wrinehill, 11/62. Sold to Broadway Coaches, Broadway, 5/64, resold to Edwards Brothers (Amalgamated), Beddau, 8/64. Briefly used, but sold for scrap 10/64.

STC4/40/78 Sentinel STC4/E
See entry for STC4/40/74.

STC4/40/79 Sentinel STC4/40 Sentinel B40F
Delivered to Morrison, Tenby, 8/51, as NDE 555, f/n 33. Sold to Cowley (dealer), Salford, 11/58. Resold to Bellis, Buckley (Mold), 12/58. Sold to Hulley, Baslow, 7/59 as f/n 16. According to one correspondent the seating capacity was increased by Hulley to B44F but we reserve judgement on this. Withdrawn from use 3/64 and sold to Hadley Trading (dealer), Wolverhampton, for scrap.

STC6/44/80 Sentinel STC6/44 Sentinel B44F
Ordered by Leon, Finningley, but cancelled before delivery. Sold to Simmons (Reliance Coaches), Great Gonerby, 6/52, as GCT 181. Sold to Roys, Nottingham, 12/62, and then to Yeates (dealer), Loughborough, 12/64. Sold to a Reverend Waddington the same month and converted into a mobile church. Reported in use as such in the Leicester and Bristol areas during 1965 but no sightings after 8/65 and believed to be in Heaven.

STC6/44/81 Sentinel STC6/44 Sentinel B44F
Registered to Sentinel (Shrewsbury) 3/52 as HUJ 619 and used as a demonstrator before delivery to Whieldon's Green Bus, Rugeley, 4/53 as f/n 42. Sold to Riviera Services, Mylor Bridge, 1/57 and initially registered to subsidiary company Lewis, of Falmouth. Withdrawn from service 3/65 and next reported converted into a flat-bed stock-car transporter at Exmouth in 2/66. Owner and ultimate fate unknown.

STC6/44/82 Sentinel STC6/44 Sentinel B44F
Registered to Sentinel (Shrewsbury) 6/51 as HAW 577 and used as a demonstrator before sale to Camplejohn Brothers, Darfield, 3/52 as f/n 28. Business sold to Yorkshire Traction, Barnsley, 1/61 and vehicle taken over as f/n 129C. Sold to North (dealer), Leeds, 2/63 and then resold to Tumilty (AA Motor Services), Ayr, 5/63. Withdrawn from service 5/66 and sold to Codona (dealer), Paisley, 7/66 for scrap.

STC4/40/83 Sentinel STC4/40 Sentinel B40F
Believed completed in 1952 and placed into store. Delivered to Trimdon Motor Services

Above: The Greenwich operator Lewis had an eye for the unusual and had tried Fodens before turning to Sentinel. Duple Elizabethan-bodied **OXT 23** was the first of three basically similar SLC6/30s which gave good service well into the 1960s and is seen on the final approaches to Epsom racetrack. After a second career in Snowdonia it ended its days in Kent serving an unknown purpose at a boarding kennels.

Below: Trimdon Motor Services operated STC4/40s, STC6/44s, an SLC4/35, two SLC4/27s and two SLC6/30s with Associated Coach Builders Coronation Land Cruiser bodywork. This is the second, **PPT 850**. Both carried Bluebird fleetnames but were registered to the parent company.

4/54 as OUP 582, f/n 26. F/n changed to 22 in 12/55. Sold to Hughes (dealer), Bradford, 10/60 and then resold to Craiggs, Amble, in 12/60. Sold to Appleby (Terrier Coaches), Choppington, 10/63. Withdrawn from service 1/64 and sold for scrap 6/64.

STC4/40/84 Sentinel STC4/40 Sentinel B40F
Believed completed in 1952 and placed into store. Delivered to Trimdon Motor Services 8/54 as OUP 580, f/n 10. Sold to Hughes (dealer), Bradford, 10/60. Sold to Phillips Coach Company, Shiptonthorpe, 8/61, as f/n 35. Withdrawn from service 11/63 and derelict by 4/65. Later scrapped.

STC4/40/85 Sentinel STC4/40 Brewery delivery vehicle
Last vehicle from STC4/40 production line and converted into a goods vehicle using many components from the standard bus model, including the entire front end. Delivered via North Cheshire Motors (distributor), Stockton Heath, to Greenall Whitley, Warrington, 6/51 as HED 480, f/n 26. Last sighting in brewery livery in 1955. Next noted operating as a dropside coal lorry in Liverpool 10/63 and ultimate fate unknown.

SLC6/42/86 Sentinel SLC6/42 Brewery delivery vehicle
Exported at an unknown date (possibly 1952) to British Engineering & Appliances (distributor), Adelaide, Australia. One of two SLC6/42s equipped with goods bodywork to the order of Tooth's Brewery, Sydney. Registration and fate unknown.

STC6/44/87 Sentinel STC6/44 Sentinel B44F
Delivered to Boyer, Rothley, 6/51, as GUT 543. Business acquired by BMMO (Midland Red) 1/59 and vehicle retained as f/n 4847 (also catalogued by body number BB4840). Sold for scrap after accident damage 7/61.

STC6/44/88 Sentinel STC6/44 Sentinel B44F
Delivered to Duggins (Princess Bus Service), Newcastle-under-Lyme, 9/51 as VRF 822, f/n 1. Operator changed name by marriage to Belshaw in 1965, still trading as Princess. Sold to a scrap dealer after engine seized in 4/67.

STC6/44/89 Sentinel STC6/44 Sentinel B44F
Delivered to Camplejohn Brothers, Darfield, 6/52 as LWT 880, f/n 29. Business acquired by Yorkshire Traction, Barnsley, 1/61 and vehicle became YTC f/n 130C. Sold to North (dealer), Leeds 2/63 and then resold to Gaile (AA Motor Services), Irvine, 5/63. Withdrawn from service 7/66 and scrapped on site by operator.

STC6/44/90 Sentinel STC6/44 Sentinel B44F
Delivered to Edwards Brothers Motors, Crymmych, 2/52, as ODE 182. Business sold in 1957, becoming Rees and Phillips (Midway Motors) and vehicle repainted accordingly. Withdrawn from service 5/63 and placed into open storage at depot. In use as a storage unit by 10/74, and derelict by 5/85. Rescued by Bowers, Sunningdale, for preservation in 1990 and moved to a site near Ascot. Sold to Hinchliffe (preservationist), Huddersfield, in 1998 and currently under restoration at the premises of the Huddersfield Passenger Transport Group.

STC6/44/91 Sentinel STC4/44 Sentinel B44F
Some reports give the c/n as STC4/44/91. Experimental prototype combining a 4-cylinder 4SRH2/4D engine with the underframe and bodywork units of a 44-seat vehicle. Registered to Sentinel (Shrewsbury) in 6/51 as HAW 578 and used as a development vehicle for the new direct injection engines and as an occasional demonstrator. Sold to Boyer, Rothley, 4/53. Business acquired by BMMO (Midland Red) 1/59 and vehicle became f/n 4846 (BMMO body number BB4839). Sold to Large (dealer), Bilston, 7/63, and then to Hazeldine, Bilston, 10/63. According to one report Hazeldine replaced the vehicle's Sentinel engine with a BMMO 8-litre unit previously used in an S10 present at the Large dealership at the same time, but this remains unconfirmed. Withdrawn from use 7/64 and later scrapped on site.

STC6/44/92 Sentinel STC6/44 Sentinel B44F
Delivered to Roberts (Pioneer), Newport (Pembrokeshire) 5/52. Sold to Duggins (Princess Bus Service), Newcastle-under-Lyme, f/n 2, 4/54. Operator changed name to Belshaw by marriage in 1965. Withdrawn from service in 3/69 and sold for scrap.

Above: To most observers the Land Cruiser's attractiveness as top-dressing for a Sentinel was rivalled only by that of the Whitson Grand Prix design. This is **GJR 965** in service with its original owner, Longstaff, of Morpeth in Northumberland.

Below: Another Grand Prix, this one the famous **JTL 469** of Simmons, of Great Gonerby near Grantham. This vehicle was frequently sighted in Blackpool, the Lake District, Scarborough, and even Torquay, during its high-mileage career with Simmons who traded as Reliance Coaches. The livery is red and cream.

STC6/44/93 Sentinel STC6/44 Sentinel B44F
Delivered to Whieldon's Green Bus, Rugeley, 5/53, as YRF 732, f/n 43. Sold to Riviera Services, Mylor Bridge, 10/57. Withdrawn from service 5/62 and used as spares for STC6/44/81 and STC6/44/99. The vehicle's remains are believed to have been scrapped on site.

STC6/44/94 Sentinel STC6/44 Sentinel B44F
Originally ordered by Leon, Finningley, and registration NNN 998 booked on their behalf by Sentinel in 6/52. Cancelled shortly before delivery and vehicle diverted (still with its Nottinghamshire registration, as favoured by Leon) to Owen, Upper Boddington, in 8/52. Sold to Trimdon Motor Services 10/57 as f/n 11. Withdrawn from service by 5/59 after an engine failure and sold to Hughes (dealer), Bradford, who fitted it with a 4-cylinder unit salvaged from an unknown SLC4/35. Passed on to Cowdell (dealer), Newport (Mon) 4/61 and then resold to Elmes (Jordans Motors), Blaenavon 5/61. Withdrawn from service and noted engineless at the depot 4/62. Sold to Cowley (dealer), Salford and in use with Norwest Construction as a site hut at their Liverpool yard by 6/63. Ultimate fate unknown but last noted in very poor condition.

STC6/44/95 Sentinel STC6/44 Sentinel B44F
Exhibited at Commercial Motor Show 10/50 in pseudo-Ribble livery complete with bogus f/n 266 applied in Ribble style. Registered to Sentinel (Shrewsbury) as GUX 614 and used as a demonstrator from 3/51, retaining its Motor Show livery. Sold to Llynfi Motors, Maesteg, 3/52 as f/n 63 (but still with '266' on the internal bulkhead). Sold to Don Everall (dealer), Wolverhampton, 12/58, and then resold to Wotton (contractor), Wombwell, 2/59. Sold to Hargreaves, Darfield, 5/62. Sold to Kirkby (dealer), South Anston, 5/63 and then passed on to Hedges (dealer), Fair Oak. Sold for scrap 1/64.

SLC6/42/96 Sentinel SLC6/42 Brewery delivery vehicle
Delivered to British Engineering & Appliances, Adelaide. See entry for SLC6/42/86

STC6/44/97 Sentinel STC6/44 Sentinel B44F
Delivered to Whieldon's Green Bus, Rugeley, 5/53, as YRF 733, f/n 44. Sold to Riviera Services, Mylor Bridge, 10/57. Sold to Trimdon Motor Services 6/58 as f/n 26 (not to be confused with STC4/40/83 which also bore this fleet number). Sold to Hughes (dealer), Bradford, 9/60 and then immediately resold to Milson, Coningsby. Sold to Don Everall (dealer), Wolverhampton, 1/62 and then resold to Powell, Ellesmere Port, 3/62. Withdrawn from use in 1/63 and next reported in 10/64, operating as a mobile shop on the Wirral peninsula with a Mr Ray. Fate unknown, but no further sightings after 1964.

STC6/44/98 Sentinel STC6/44 Sentinel B44F
Delivered to Davies Brothers, Pencader, 1/52, as GTH 576. Withdrawn from use 7/54 and sold to Llynfi Motors, Maesteg, as f/n 64. Sold to Don Everall (dealer), Wolverhampton, 2/59 and then resold to Campion (Princess Bus Service), Clonmel, Ireland, in 3/59. Sold to Regan (dealer), Dublin, 5/65 and then immediately resold to Star Minibus Transport, Dublin. Returned to Regan 5/66 and then resold shortly afterwards to Leonard, Malahide, who seems to have been a private individual rather than an operator or dealer. No further reports but rumours persist that this vehicle may survive in long-term storage, with one correspondent mentioning a second career as a motor-caravan in 1967/8. Given the sad fate of SLC4/35/56 we should very much like to find this vehicle - if it still exists.

STC6/44/99 Sentinel STC6/44 Sentinel B44F
Delivered to Whieldon's Green Bus, Rugeley, 5/53, as YRF 734, f/n 45. Sold to Riviera Services, Mylor Bridge, 1/58. Withdrawn from service 9/64 and sold to Tudor Williams (Pioneer), Laugharne, 4/65. Withdrawn by them in 7/66 and subsequent fate unknown.

STC6/44/100 Sentinel STC6/44 Sentinel B44F
Registered to Sentinel (Shrewsbury) 3/53 as JNT 763. Intended as a demonstrator but the model it represented was discontinued within months of its completion. Sold to Trimdon Motor Services 2/54 and reregistered OUP 578 upon repaint into fleet livery as f/n 4. Sold to Hughes (dealer), Bradford, 10/60, and then resold to Baddeley Brothers, Holmfirth, 11/60

Above: Hoare, of Chickerell, near Weymouth, was one of three Sentinel customers who traded under the Bluebird name (the other two were Trimdon and a Hull coach operator). This is their Duple Elizabethan-bodied SLC6/30, **GTK 992**, operating a private hire for naval personnel bound for Portsmouth.

Below: Schofield, of Marsden, near Huddersfield, bought four SLC6/30s in early 1955 and had them equipped with Burlingham Seagull bodywork. This is the first of the four, **OWU 771**, and was photographed while participating in the Clacton Coach Rally. The Schofield business was sold to Hanson in 1961.

as f/n 62. Withdrawn from use in 1/65, and then sold to Haigh (dealer), Huddersfield, 5/65, and scrapped.

SLC6/41/101 Sentinel SLC6/41 Plaxton Venturer C41C (1860)
Delivered to Warner Motors, Tewkesbury, 4/52 as LDF 296. Withdrawn from use 9/60 and sold to Talbott (Barry's Coaches), Moreton-in-the-Marsh, 11/60. Resold the same month to Don Everall (dealer), Wolverhampton, and then resold to Brown (Falcon Coaches), Baillieston, 12/60. Returned to Everall 4/62 and then sold to Prance, Cardiff, 8/63. Returned to Everall 10/63 and then sold to Dudley, Inkberrow, 12/63. Back to Everall 1/64 and immediately resold to Rowe (Cray Coaches), St. Pauls Cray. Returned to Everall 1/65 and scrapped during 1966.

SLC6/41/102 Sentinel SLC6/41 Bellhouse-Hartwell Landmaster C32C
Incorrectly plated as SLC6/44/102. Exhibited at Commercial Motor Show, 10/52, in livery of Smiths Tours, Wigan, but never delivered to them. Sold to Blue Cars, London WC2, 4/53 as NLR 850. Sold to Cowley (dealer), Salford, 12/61, and then resold (via Dunchurch yard) to Moore (Glider Coaches), Great Witley, 7/62. Layout changed to C34C whilst with Moore. Withdrawn from use 8/67 and scrapped on site during 1969.

Construction numbers 103-109 Not completed. See Note 2.

SLC6/42/110 Sentinel SLC6/42 ???? B49D
Chassis only exported to Ceylon (now Sri Lanka) 1/53 and fitted with local bodywork by an unknown manufacturer. First registered to Fernando (dealer), Colombo, as IC 1467. Acquired by Colombo Omnibus Company later in 1953, and that business acquired by Ceylon Transport Board in 1958. Withdrawn from service in 1966 and scrapped.

Construction numbers 111-112 Not completed. See Note 2.

SLC6/42/113 Sentinel SLC6/42 Bellhouse-Hartwell Landmaster C32CT
Originally intended for Drake Expeditions, Buenos Aires, Argentina, where it would have been fitted with locally built bodywork for tours to southern Patagonia, but never delivered. Fitted with a C32CT body (including toilet compartment) 7/52 and then delivered to Blue Cars, London WC2, 10/52 as MYV 637 after display at the Commercial Motor Show. Normally based at Boulogne, France, although remaining under UK registry throughout until withdrawn from use at the end of the 1960 touring season. Sold to Cowley (dealer), Salford, 5/61 and then resold to Lipsey (Mandator Coaches), Northolt 8/61 for use on overland tours to Greece and India. Its actual use on these activities remains unconfirmed as the UK licensing record terminates with the sale to Lipsey and there were no further sightings of the vehicle. It could possibly have been licensed overseas but it seems more likely that it was scrapped.

Second Series

4271 Sentinel SLC4/27 (JCB 139) Beadle C35C (C331)
Originally intended for Grainger (Eagle Coaches), Smethwick, but cancelled before delivery and placed in store by Beadle after completion in late 1953. Sold to Chapple, Raglan, 4/55, as NWO 122. Withdrawn from service 2/64 but remained in open storage at the depot until sold to Buckland (scrap dealer), Golden Valley, Gloucestershire, circa 1967. Became semi-derelict, but rescued 3/73 by Messrs Wheatley of Kenilworth, and Perry of Bromyard (preservationists). Currently stored at a private location in Herefordshire.

4272 Sentinel SLC4/27 (JCB 138) Beadle C35C (C330)
Originally intended for Grainger (Eagle Coaches), Smethwick, but cancelled before delivery and placed in store by Beadle after completion in 10/53. Sold to Back, Witney, 5/54 as HBW 505. Withdrawn from use during 1962 and sold to Watling Street Motors (dealer), Redbourne, for scrap.

4273 Sentinel SLC4/27 (JCB 140) Beadle C35C (C332)
Delivered to Trimdon Motor Services 4/54 as PPT 213, f/n 9. Operated in Bluebird Coaches

Above: When Sentinel ceased production three unsold SLC6/33 chassis passed to Tom Ward's Transport Vehicles Warrington company (TVW) and were completed as goods vehicles. This is the second of the three, **704 HTB**, which ended up as a cattle transporter with haulier Jones, of Urmston (just outside Manchester). This is a TVW shot taken at the Congleton premises of Boalloy who built lorry cab shells for both TVW and nearby Cheshire chassis maker ERF.

Below: The very last SLC6/30 was also the last Sentinel PSV. Originally ordered by Wallace Arnold Sales and Service, it was cancelled when already in build at Blackpool where Burlingham equipped it with this Seagull body. Its eventual purchaser was Bengry, of Leominster, trading as Primrose Coaches, who registered it as **NVJ 664**. The vehicle is seen here at an unidentified football-ground, wearing Primrose's yellow and cream livery.

livery although never officially owned by that TMS subsidiary (this proviso applies to all the TMS coach-bodied Sentinels). Withdrawn from use 7/60 and sold to Hughes (dealer), Bradford. Sold to Daisy Bus Service, Broughton (Lincs), 9/60. Withdrawn from service 12/61 and sold to Dorman (dealer), Bunny (Notts), 5/62 for scrapping.

4274 Sentinel SLC4/27 (JCB 141) Beadle C35C (C333)
Delivered to Trimdon Motor Services 4/54 as PPT 214, f/n 7. Withdrawn from use 7/60 and sold to Hughes (dealer), Bradford. Passed on to Cowdell (dealer), Newport (Mon) 8/60, but remained unsold and passed back to Hughes 11/60. Sold to Valley Supply, Bacup, 12/60, for use as a mobile shop. Sold to Mills, Stacksteads, in early 1964 for continued use as a mobile shop, but by 21/7/64 was derelict in a field alongside the main road from Halifax to Leeds. Scrapped soon afterwards.

4301 Sentinel SLC4/30 ???? B56D
Assembled from SLC4/35 components with lengthened front and rear chassis members and then exported to Ceylon in 1954 and fitted with locally built bodywork. The seating capacity seems unlikely but is quoted as reported. We suspect that the figure may include the number of standees allowed. Sold to the Colombo Omnibus Company as IC 2191 3/54 and passed with that business to the Ceylon Transport Board in 1958. Withdrawn from service during 1966 and believed scrapped.

6301 Sentinel SLC6/30 (no known bodywork)
Completed in 3/53. Originally intended for Pritchard, Narberth, but cancelled before being fitted with bodywork. Retained for development purposes until early 1954 and then exported via Cranwood (shipping agent) to South Africa. Later reported with pantechnicon bodywork, operating as a furniture removal van with Massons Cartage, Randfontein. South African registration and ultimate fate unknown.

6302 Sentinel SLC6/30 Plaxton Venturer C37C (2114)
Delivered to Partridge (Bantam Coaches), Coventry, 3/53 as MKV 607. Sold to Appleford (LEA Coaches) by 8/56 and then resold to Hart (Cosy Coaches), Donisthorpe, 1/57. Converted to C41C configuration while with Hart. Sold to Ementon, Cranfield 3/60 and then resold to Margo, Bexleyheath 10/61. Derelict in yard by 1964 and believed scrapped.

6303 Sentinel SLC6/30 Plaxton Venturer C41C (2189)
Completed 9/53 and originally intended for Bristol Co-operative Society (Queen of the Road), Fishponds, Bristol, as RHW 233. Delivery postponed until 4/54, original marks allowed to lapse, and reregistered as SHT 468 before entering service as f/n 40. Sold to Warner Motors, Tewkesbury, 4/63 and then resold 2/64 to Moore (Glider Coaches), Great Witley, although not licenced by them until 9/65. Withdrawn from use in 1969 and scrapped on site during 1970.

6304 Sentinel SLC6/30 Burlingham Seagull Mk.3 C41C (5718)
Delivered to Wallace Arnold (distributor), Leeds, 2/54 as SUG 19 and used as a demonstrator before delivery to Metcalfe, Keighley, 5/54. Hired back by Wallace Arnold to give rides from the demonstration park at the Commercial Motor Show 10/54. Sold to Steel, Addingham, 5/57, and resold to Jones (Doug's Coaches), Pitt, Hampshire, 1/59. Sold to Kemp, Chillenden, Kent 2/59, and withdrawn by them 1/62. Next reported with Downing & Wenham (Eastbourne Coachways), Eastbourne 5/63. Sold via a dealership in Battle to Dowell, Burwash, 3/64, and then sold on to Waterhouse Coaches, Burwash in 11/64. Sold to John Gords Coaches, Framfield 4/66, and then to Denyer Brothers, Stondon, 5/66. Withdrawn from use by 1970 and next reported when found in poor condition in a corner of Denyer's yard in 1990. Rescued in 9/01 by Plant (preservationist), Sale, and then resold to Wheatley (preservationist), Kenilworth, 10/01. Currently stored, still in poor condition, at a private location in Herefordshire.

6305 Sentinel SLC6/30 Duple Elizabethan C41C (187/1)
Delivered to C G Lewis (Greenwich) Ltd, London SE10, in 3/54 as OXT 23. Sold to Roberts, Llanberis, in 8/64. No sightings with

Above: This STC6/44, **LWT 880**, was delivered to Camplejohn Brothers and passed with the business to Yorkshire Traction who fitted this ugly roof-box to it before selling it on for further service in Ayrshire with AA Motor Services.

Below: One of the last STC6/44s in regular stage-carriage use was **OUP 578**, which endeared itself to enthusiasts by ending up operating in the attractive Holmfirth area in the colourful fleet of Baddeley Brothers . Built as a Sentinel demonstrator (and first registered JNT 763) it ran for Trimdon Motor Services before joining Baddeley in 1960. They kept it in use until 1965.

Roberts after 1966 and next reported with Redsheen Kennels, Tunbridge Wells, 12/71 serving in an unspecified non-PSV role (possibly as a dog bus). No further reports.

6306 Sentinel SLC6/30 Duple Elizabethan C41C (196/2)
Registered to Sentinel (Shrewsbury) 2/54 as KUJ 141 for use as a demonstrator. Sold to Bluebird Garages, Hull, in 6/54. Sold to Carrs Coaches, New Silksworth, (County Durham), 2/56. Sold to Foster, Easington Colliery, 12/64 and then to Hylton Castle Coaches, Sunderland 12/66. No further reports after 1967.

6307 Sentinel SLC6/30 A.C.B. B42D
Registered to Sentinel (Shrewsbury) 5/54 as KUX 412 for use as a demonstrator by K.B. Motors (distributor), Newcastle-upon-Tyne. Sold to Moffit, Acomb, later in 1954, still in dual-door configuration. Sold to Llynfi Motors, Maesteg, 2/55 as f/n 65, by then converted to single-door B44F layout. It is unclear who was responsible for this conversion. Sold to Don Everall (dealer), Wolverhampton, 1/60, and then resold to Simpson, Cardenden, 8/60. Withdrawn from use 7/63 and scrapped 10/63.

6308 Sentinel SLC6/30 Whitson B44F
Delivered to Simmons (Reliance Coaches), Great Gonerby, in 1/54 as HCT 618. Withdrawn from service 9/61 and retained as a source of spares for STC6/44/80 and 63020. Remains scrapped at depot by 12/64.

6309 Sentinel SLC6/30 Duple Elizabethan C41C (196/1)
Delivered to C.G. Lewis (Greenwich) Ltd, London SE10 in 3/54 as OXT 24. Sold to Seth, London NW5, 6/66. Withdrawn from use 3/67 and used as a source of spares for PXE 761 (63013). No further reports after 10/67, presumed scrapped.

63010 Sentinel SLC6/30 A.C.B. Coronation Land Cruiser C39C
Delivered to Trimdon Motor Services 7/54 as PPT 850, f/n 39. Converted to C41C configuration while with Trimdon. Withdrawn from service 9/60 and sold to Hughes (dealer), Bradford. Sold to Letham, Blantyre, 1/61. Withdrawn from use 5/62 and placed into open storage. Sold to Tumilty (AA Motor Services), Ayr, 4/65 as spares for STC6/44/82 and STC6/44/89. Remains scrapped 5/65.

63011 Sentinel SLC6/30 A.C.B. Coronation Land Cruiser C41C
Delivered to Trimdon Motor Services 6/54 as PPT 690, f/n 3. Withdrawn from service 7/60 and sold to Hughes (dealer), Bradford. Sold to Gott, Bradford, 8/60. Returned to Hughes in early 1962 and then sold to Batterby (scrap dealer), Royton, by 4/62.

63012 Sentinel SLC6/30 Burlingham B44F
Exhibited on the Burlingham stand at the Commercial Motor Show 10/54 in the livery of Whieldon's Green Bus, Rugeley, and delivered to them 2/55 as 775 ERF, f/n 47. Sold to Camplejohn Brothers, Darfield, 3/57 as f/n 33. Business acquired by Yorkshire Traction, Barnsley, 1/61 and vehicle became YTC f/n 132C. Sold to Mellor, Gloxhill, 12/64. Sold to Peter Sheffield, Cleethorpes, 5/67 as f/n 34. Withdrawn from use 9/69 and later scrapped.

63013 Sentinel SLC6/30 Duple Elizabethan C41C (215/1)
Originally intended for Wiggs (Grey Coaches), London SE15, but cancelled before delivery after takeover of Wiggs by Banfield. Exhibited on the Sentinel stand at the Commercial Motor Show, 10/54, in the livery of C.G. Lewis (Greenwich) Ltd, London SE10, and delivered to them in 1/55 as PXE 761. Sold to Seth, London NW5, 6/66. Sold to L.C.M. (dealer), Dunstable, 10/67. Next reported in 1971 after conversion to a stock-car transporter, operating for Simpson Engineering, Brixham. Sold to Jolly, East Boldre (Hants), by 3/81 and then to Bronson, Bristol, by 1990. Sold to Spiers, Henley-on-Thames in 1995 for preservation. Last reported roadworthy and in good condition, albeit still in stock-car configuration with rear-end loading doors.

63014 Sentinel SLC6/30 Whitson Grand Prix C37C
Delivered to Longstaff, Broomhill, 6/54, as GJR 965. Reported withdrawn 1962 but noted operating with Pickering (Doreen's Coaches), Blackhall Rocks, 10/67. No further reports and presumed scrapped after tax expiry in 10/68.

Above: The Birmingham and Midland Motor Omnibus Company (alias Midland Red) preferred its own underfloor designs, but found itself in possession of two Sentinel STC6/44s through the acquisition of Boyer, Rothley. This one is **HAW 578** (BMMO fleet number **4846**), seen between duties in Leicester. The vehicle had briefly been a Sentinel demonstrator and had been experimentally fitted with a 4-cylinder 4SRH2 engine, which it retained throughout its careers with Boyer and Midland Red. Subsequent owner Hazeldine, of Bilston, found this unacceptable and fitted it with an 8-litre BMMO powerplant retrieved from a Midland Red S10.

Below: Boyer's other STC6/44 came straight off the production line and was registered **GUT 543** by the Leicestershire operator. The vehicle is seen here in St. Margarets bus station, Leicester, while operating Boyer's frequent stage service, but at weekends both vehicles could often be found at the seaside with Blackpool and Skegness their favourite destinations. Meanwhile Boyer's solitary STC4/40 and a Bedford SB service bus would cover the local route.

63015 Sentinel SLC6/30 Whitson Grand Prix C41C
New to Hastelow, Malvern, 8/54, as NAB 756. Withdrawn from use 11/61. Sold to Thomas (Swanbrook Coaches), Staverton, 5/62. Withdrawn 11/67 and scrapped by 2/68.

63016 Sentinel SLC6/30 Plaxton Venturer C41C (2392)
Allocated to Wallace Arnold (distributor), Leeds, and registration SUG 17 reserved but not used. Delivered by them to Bluebird Garages, Hull, in 6/54 as RAT 645. Sold to P. & M. Coach Line, Ipswich, 6/57 as f/n 51. Sold to Cook, Braintree, 6/64, then resold to Cutting, Brockley, 10/64. Sold to Arlington (dealer), Sudbury, by 5/66, but remained unsold and later scrapped.

63017 Sentinel SLC6/30 Whitson B44F
Exhibited on the Whitson stand at the Commercial Motor Show 10/54 in the livery of Draytonian Coaches, Yiewsley, Middlesex, but never operated by them and served as a Whitson demonstrator (operating on trade plates) until sale to Warner Motors, Tewkesbury, 8/56, as SDF 17. Sold to Talbott (Barry's Coaches), Moreton-in-the-Marsh, 1/60. Withdrawn from service 12/65 and sold to Evans (dealer), Wellington, Shropshire. Next reported at Bilston 6/66, converted into a stock-car transporter. No further sightings.

63018 Sentinel SLC6/30 Whitson Grand Prix C41C
Delivered to Bristol Co-operative Society (Queen of the Road), Fishponds, Bristol, 7/54, as TAE 618, f/n 39. Sold to Warner Motors, Tewkesbury, 5/63, resold to Broadway Coaches, Broadway, 12/63. Withdrawn early 1966, sold to Southern Counties Car Auctions (dealer), Farnham, 4/66. No further trace.

63019 Sentinel SLC6/30 Whitson DP44F
This vehicle has been identified in some publications as the vehicle in Draytonian livery at the 1954 Motor Show, but this is clearly incorrect (see 63017). Registered to Rees & Williams, Tycroes, in 7/54 as KBX 630. In service with them (in full R & W livery) on a daily basis throughout the Show in question. Sold to Peters, Pembrey, 10/66, and then resold to O'Neil, Llanelli, by 7/67. No further reports and presumed scrapped.

63020 Sentinel SLC6/30 Whitson Grand Prix C40C
Delivered to Simmons (Reliance Coaches), Great Gonerby, 5/55, as JTL 469. Withdrawn from service 5/65 and scrapped on site 2/66.

63021 Sentinel SLC6/30 Duple Elizabethan C41C (215/2)
Delivered to Hoare (Bluebird Coaches), Chickerell, 11/54, as GTK 992. Withdrawn from use 11/63 and no further reports.

63022 Sentinel SLC6/30 Burlingham Seagull Mk 2 C37C
Allocated to Wallace Arnold (distributor), Leeds, and exhibited in their livery on the Sentinel stand at the Commercial Motor Show, 10/54. Registered UUB 931 in 3/55 and used as a demonstrator before transfer to the Wallace Arnold Tours fleet later in the same year. Sold to Hughes (dealer), Bradford, 11/62. Sold to Thornton, Shaw (Lancs) 6/63, returned to Hughes 7/63, and then resold to Lamb, Malton, 7/64. Withdrawn from use in 10/65 and then sold back to Hughes 8/66. No further reports.

63023 Sentinel SLC6/30 Whitson Grand Prix C40C
Exhibited on the Whitson stand at the Commercial Motor Show, 10/54, in the livery of Cowell, Sunderland, but never operated by them and delivered immediately after the show to Best & Son, Wembley, as 657 CMT. Shown in tax records as sold to L.C.M. (dealer), Dunstable, 12/63, but by 4/64 operating for Willesden Coaches, London NW (also owned by the Best family), so this may have been a paper transaction in connection with a hire-purchase deal. Sold to Smith, Leighton Buzzard, by 8/65 for an unspecified non-PSV use, with differing reports of its conversion to either a stock-car transporter or a motor caravan. No further sightings, although this vehicle was mistakenly listed as still with Willesden Coaches in the 1966/7 editions of the Little Red Book.

63024 Sentinel SLC6/30 Burlingham Seagull Mk 2 C41C (5930)

Above: STC4/40 **GUJ 608** served as a demonstrator until it became obvious that the model's reputation was irretrievably sullied and was then sold to private-hire operator Leader, of London E15 (trading as Maryland Coaches). From there it went to Warner, of Tewkesbury, and then to Brown, of Donnington Wood. The vehicle is seen here in service with Browns at Wellington bus station in Shropshire. It is currently preserved.

Below: Browns were more famous for their Beadle-bodied SLC4/35s, taking five new examples and then buying a former demonstrator. In the mid-1960s several of these were modified to make them more suitable for the Telford Rota routes and for one-man operation. This involved moving the entrance door to the front and expanding the seating capacity, in some cases by as many as six, by using bus seats in place of coach units. **HNT 49** received the full modification and is seen here after retirement, in the company of trolleybuses and a Blackpool PD2/5 at Sandtoft. It is still preserved.

Delivered to Schofield, Marsden, 1/55 as OWU 771. Business acquired by Smith, Marsden, 4/58 (still trading as Schofield). Sold to Gee Cross Motors, Hyde, 3/60. Business acquired by Kitson, Stalybridge, 8/60 but Gee Cross trading name retained although garage closed and all vehicles kept at Stalybridge. Last reported 10/66 and fate unknown.

63025 Sentinel SLC6/30 Burlingham Seagull Mk 2 C41C (5931)
Delivered to Schofield, Marsden, 2/55 as OWU 772. Business acquired by Smith, Marsden, 4/58 (still trading as Schofield). Business acquired by Hanson, Huddersfield 12/61. Vehicle sold to Hughes (dealer), Bradford, 3/64 and then resold to Lamb, Malton, 6/64. Withdrawn from use 2/69 and believed scrapped.

63026 Sentinel SLC6/30 Burlingham Seagull Mk 2 C41C (5932)
Delivered to Schofield, Marsden, 3/55 as OWU 773. Business acquired by Smith, Marsden, 4/58 (still trading as Schofield). Business acquired by Hanson, Huddersfield 12/61. Vehicle sold to Hughes (dealer), Bradford, 2/65, and then resold to Boyes, Low Moor, 4/65. Sold to Pearson, Heywood (Lancs), 12/65. No longer owned by this operator by 9/66 and no further sightings.

63027 Sentinel SLC6/30 Burlingham Seagull Mk 2 C41C (5933)
Delivered to Schofield, Marsden, 3/55 as OWU 774. Business acquired by Smith, Marsden, 4/58 (still trading as Schofield). Business acquired by Hanson, Huddersfield 12/61. Sold to Hughes (dealer), Bradford, 11/62 and then resold within weeks to Hutchinson Brothers, Husthwaite. Sold to Pemberton, Upton, 6/65. Withdrawn by them in 10/65 and no further reports.

63028 Sentinel SLC6/30 Burlingham Seagull Mk 3 C41C (6058)
Delivered to Benyon, Atherton, 4/55 as VTB 482. Sold to K. &. B. Motors (dealer), Newcastle-upon-Tyne, in 4/56 and resold the same year to Sunbeam Coaches, North Shields. Sold to Best & Son, Wembley, 3/60. Sold to L.C.M. (dealer), Dunstable, 4/63 and then resold to Tilley (Waverley Coaches), St. Albans, 9/63. Withdrawn from use in 3/64 and no further reports.

63029 Sentinel SLC6/30 Burlingham Seagull Mk 3 C41C (6072)
Allocated to Wallace Arnold (distributor), Leeds, but delivery declined 6/55 and returned to Shrewsbury, still unregistered (this is from an official Sentinel document). At this point the vehicle appears to have vanished without trace, Seagull bodywork and all, and despite years of research has evaded capture. We do have a reliable report of an unidentified SLC6/30 with Seagull bodywork being displayed on the Hardwicks tours stand in Scarborough in 8/55, wearing basic WA livery and mock-up registration plates 'LUX 41'. The real recipient of this registration was a motorcycle, and the Sentinel in question disappeared within days, so we are unable to confirm that this was indeed 63029 (note the conflict with the date officially returned to Shrewsbury). We admit to being mystified as the vehicle was less than a year old when it vanished. Does somebody have a brand-new Sentinel hidden in a barn somewhere ?

63030 Sentinel SLC6/30 Burlingham Seagull Mk 3 C41C (6073)
Allocated to Wallace Arnold (distributor), Leeds, but cancelled before delivery and stored after completion in 11/55. Sold to Bengry (Primrose), Leominster, 4/56 as NVJ 664. Sold to Les Gleave (dealer), Arclid, 3/62, and used in service on hire to associated company, Roberts Coaches, Crewe. Sold to an unknown operator in the London area by 1963, resold to a dealer, and then vandalised whilst in the dealer's yard (details unknown). Presumed scrapped.

6331 Sentinel SLC6/33 Brewery delivery vehicle
Exported at an unknown date (possibly 1957) to British Engineering & Appliances (distributor), Adelaide, Australia. The first of four SLC6/33s with goods bodywork for Tooth's Brewery, Sydney, which had previously bought similar SLC6/42/86 and SLC6/42/96. As with the earlier vehicles, registration and fate unknown.

76

Upper: Rear ends on display in Telford New Town, showing an aspect of Sentinels often missed by photographers. The STC4/40 shows off its rear route number box, painted out by Browns and used by very few operators of the type, while the SLC4/35 emphasises the dated nature of the Beadle coach body which had much more in common with half-cab designs than those then current for underfloor-engined vehicles. Browns, however, operated Vulcans, compared to which most things looked modern.

Centre: The West Riding operator Camplejohn Brothers knew what they wanted and chose Sentinels and Atkinsons instead of AECs or Leylands. Enthusiasts mourned their passing as their attractive brown, green, and cream livery gave way to Yorkshire Traction's red. This is STC6/44 **HAW 577**, another former demonstrator, seen in Barnsley before the takeover.

Lower: H A C (Harry) Claireaux took control of Partridge and Son, Layham, from his father-in-law in the mid-1950s. A few years later the company bought two Sentinels for its stage-carriage services in Suffolk, a former SLC4/35 demonstrator and this STC4/40, **JWW 316**, which had started life in the Sheffield area with Wigmore, of Dinnington.

6332 Sentinel SLC6/33 See entry for 6331.

6333 Sentinel SLC6/33 See entry for 6331.

6334 Sentinel SLC6/33 See entry for 6331.

6335 Sentinel SLC6/33 See Note 3.

6336 Sentinel SLC6/33 Livestock Transporter
Also reported as model SOT6/33 - see Note 1. Chassis sold to Transport Vehicles Warrington (TVW) in 1957 and completed as a cattle wagon. First registered to Jones, Urmston 1/59 as 704 HTB. Sold to an unidentified owner in Liverpool 2/61, and then to F. Timms & Co., Leigh, 10/65. Last licenced 12/65 and presumed scrapped.

6337 Sentinel SLC6/33 See Note 3.

Note 1: The PSV Circle publication CXB 321 gives first series construction numbers 36 and 37 as model 'SOT6/42' without explanation of how this differed from a standard SLC6/42. As no contemporary Sentinel brochures (or magazine reports) mention this model we remain unconvinced. Explanations from some that the 'SOT' prefix was an abbreviation of 'Sentinel Overseas Type' seem contrived as the SLC6/42 was already (by the fact of its length) aimed exclusively at the export market as were models SLC4/E, STC4/E, SLC6/E and STC6/E, although not all of these were actually built. Another factor to consider is that c/ns 36 and 37 were originally part of the same Brazilian order as c/ns 34 and 35 and these two were always reported as SLC6/42s. A factory warranty list prepared in December 1955 gives all four machines as such. The confusion is compounded by second series vehicle c/n 6336 which is listed in the Lancashire taxation records as an SOT6, despite being sold within the UK, while similar vehicles 6331-4 are known to have been SLC6/33s but were sold overseas. If this 'SOT' prefix was indeed an official Sentinel designation it clearly did not stand for 'Overseas Type'. Help on this will be gratefully received by the authors.

Note 2: First series construction numbers 103-9 were intended as STC6/44 bus models but remained uncompleted. The bodywork components were shipped to Whitson and used in the superstructures of SLC6/30s 6308, 63017 and 63019, with the fate of the surplus body-kits remaining unknown. The chassis components and running units were used in the construction of SLC6/30 vehicles, but this took place in a haphazard manner and no direct tie-ups were recorded. Similarly, construction numbers 111-2 were intended as SLC6/42 export models and it is almost certain that their components ended up in two or more of the SLC6/33s built for an Australian brewery.

Note 3: At the end of production three unsold 6-cylinder PSV chassis were part of the package sold to Tom Ward's TVW consortium. One of these (6336 as recorded) became a livestock transporter in Lancashire. One or both of the others, depending on the report consulted, entered service as HGVs with haulier Morgan, of Ammanford, but no details have emerged of registrations, configurations, or ultimate fates.

STAGE-CARRIAGE OPERATORS

This listing gives brief details of 71 operators known to have used Sentinel buses and/or coaches on stage carriage services available to the general public. It thus excludes operators such as Elmes (Jordans), of Blaenavon, the Phillips Coach Company, of Shiptonthorpe and Simpson, of Cardenden, whose only timetabled journeys were restricted access schools or works services. Also excluded are operators such as Dudley, of Inkberrow; Grayscroft, of Mablethorpe; Hanson, of Huddersfield; Hastelow, of Malvern; Hutchinson Brothers, of Husthwaite; Nesbit, of Somerby and Spiers of Henley-on-Thames, where no evidence exists that (coach-bodied) Sentinels were ever used on stage carriage services whilst in their possession.

Even within the bounds of this definition, Sentinels were to be found far and wide, from the well-known examples with Ribble, Riviera and Browns to lesser known specimens with operators in remote Welsh or East Anglian villages. One curious feature of the Sentinel story is the way in which individual vehicles passed between operators with hundreds of miles between them. The most extreme case involved STC4/40 AYJ 822, delivered new to Dickson of Dundee, which next went to Silver

Above: Connor and Graham operated eastwards from Hull, with stage carriage services reaching as far as Spurn Head. STC4/40 **JWF 176**, purchased new, is seen leaving Hull for Easington. After disposal by C. & G. the vehicle ended up in Pwllheli with the Jones Caelloi fleet.

Below: Davies Brothers of Pencader bought this STC6/44, **GTH 576**, in 1952, but kept it for only two years before selling it to neighbour Llynfi, of Maesteg. Five years later it was on the move again, migrating to Campion, of Clonmel in the Republic of Ireland. Rumours abound that this machine survives somewhere in rural Ireland.

Queen of Camborne in Cornwall, and from there to Pooleys of Long Sutton in Lincolnshire. Much of its total mileage must have been clocked up while being ferried between owners.

A A MOTOR SERVICES LTD, Ayr

Formed by a breakaway group of owner-drivers from the Ayrshire Bus Owners co-operative (A1 Service) who took the Ayr-Ardrossan route with them as their share of the association's assets. A second major route was developed from Ayr to Stevenston along with local services in Ayr and Irvine. By the 1960s only three of the original partners remained; Dodds, Young and Tumilty, the last of whom had taken control of Gailes Coaches in Irvine. The two STC6/44s were acquired from Yorkshire Traction and were former Camplejohn vehicles. One was registered to Mr R Tumilty while the other was officially the property of Gailes, but they were indistinguishable in livery or usage. Towards the end of the brief career of the Sentinels in Ayrshire Mr Tumilty acquired a former Trimdon Motor Services SLC6/30 coach for use as a source of spares.
Vehicles: HAW 577 (STC6/44/82), LWT 880 (STC6/44/89), PPT 850 (63010 - not used in service).

AMALGAMATED BUS SERVICES - see EDWARDS, Beddau

W M APPLEBY, Choppington, Northumberland

Appleby began a service from Morpeth to Newcastle in 1938, using various trading names until settling upon Terrier Coaches in the 1950s. The first of the Sentinels arrived in July 1962 from Service Coaches and had previously served with Moffit and then Charlton in the area to the north of Hexham. It was replaced by a second example, a former Trimdon machine, acquired from Craiggs, of Amble, in October 1963, but this vehicle was also withdrawn in early 1964. The service from Morpeth to Newcastle passed to Tyneside PTE in 1975.
Vehicles: ETY 174 (STC4/40/69), OUP 582 (STC4/40/83).

BADDELEY BROTHERS LTD, Holmfirth, West Yorkshire

Jesse and Leonard Baddeley bought their first PSV in 1919 for use on a route (soon abandoned) in the Brighouse area. Primarily a coach operator whose vehicles were seen as far away as Clacton and Torquay, either on their own tours or on hire to Yelloway, Baddeley Brothers also developed local bus services in the Holmfirth and Penistone areas. By the time of the 1930 Road Traffic Act the company was operating a route from Huddersfield to Sheffield via Holmfirth, Penistone, and Deepcar, but a licence was denied for the segment between Deepcar and Sheffield and timings between Holmfirth and Huddersfield were severely limited. This was obviously a major setback but the company persevered with its rural remnant and made a famous name for itself among ramblers and bus enthusiasts alike. The Sentinel, an STC6/44, was a former demonstrator and Trimdon Motor Services vehicle and arrived in November 1960. It lasted for just over four years by which time the hills around Holmfirth must have tested it to destruction point. The Baddeley Brothers business was sold to West Yorkshire PTE in March 1976.
Vehicle: OUP 578 (STC6/44/100) f/n 62.

BARRY'S COACHES - see TALBOTT, Moreton-in-the-Marsh.

BELSHAW - see DUGGINS, Newcastle-under-Lyme.

BIRMINGHAM & MIDLAND MOTOR OMNIBUS CO. LTD, Smethwick

There is little need to introduce BMMO, the legal title of the gigantic bus company which operated as Midland Red. The BET Group's largest operational subsidiary had a territory that extended from Hereford to Northampton and from Burton to Banbury, and became nationally renowned for its (often strange-looking) self-built vehicles. Having its own series of underfloor-engined single-decker designs, the company had no requirement for Sentinels, but in 1959 acquired two with the takeover of Boyer of Rothley. Boyer's STC4/40 had already been sold by this time, but the two STC6/44s (one fitted with a 4-cylinder engine) were duly repainted in Midland Red livery and operated from Leicester garage. One vehicle

Above: Dickson, of Dundee, was primarily a tours operator and shortly after taking delivery of this early STC4/40, **AYJ 822**, disposed of their only stage carriage service. The Sentinel was thus surplus to requirements and found its way to Mundy (Silver Queen) in far off Cornwall. The balance of the Dickson business later passed to Wallace Arnold, another company with Sentinels in its past.

Below: The partnership of Messrs Drew and Wren traded as the Castle Motor Company and operated local services in the Canterbury area. **GNT 190** was the original STC4/40 demonstrator and arrived in Kent in 1957 after several years with Whieldon's Green Bus, of Rugeley. As with the Trimdon Motor Services examples, it was replaced by a Duple (Midland)-bodied Thames Trader.

was withdrawn in 1961, but the other lasted until 1963.
Vehicles: GUT 543 (STC6/44/87) f/n 4847, HAW 578 (STC6/44/91) f/n 4846.

BLUE LINE - see MORGAN, Armthorpe.

H BOYER & COMPANY, Rothley, Leicestershire
This independent ran a daily trunk service from Leicester to Loughborough via Rothley, Mountsorrel, and Quorn, operating in competition with Housden, of Loughborough, Midland Red and Trent. Further competition along parts of the route was provided by Howlett, of Quorn, and by Barton. Boyer bought an early model STC4/40 and then two STC6/44s, one new, the other a former demonstrator with a 4-cylinder engine. In addition to stage carriage work, the Sentinels were to be seen on private-hire and excursion work in resorts as distant from Rothley as Blackpool and Skegness, although one correspondent who travelled to the Lancashire coast aboard an STC6/44 commented that the ride could have been enjoyed only by an enthusiast. The stage services, the two surviving Sentinels, and a Royal Tiger bus which had replaced the STC4/40, were sold to Midland Red in January 1959.
Vehicles: GAY 50 (STC4/40/3), GUT 543 (STC6/44/87), HAW 578 (STC6/44/91).

BROADWAY COACHES (BROADWAY) LTD, Broadway, Worcestershire
Mr Edward Harrison bought a 14-seat Chevrolet in 1929 and began a regular service from his home village of Stourton to Cheltenham. The business moved to the larger village of Broadway in the 1940s and became a limited company in 1952. An SLC6/30 was acquired third-hand in December 1963 and saw extensive use on the Cheltenham service before its sale just over two years later. Meanwhile an STC4/40 bus had been acquired in May 1964, but this proved less popular and was sold after only three months with Broadway.
Vehicles: HAW 179 (STC4/40/77), TAE 618 (63018).

H BROWN & SONS, Donnington Wood, Shropshire

This business began in 1920 when Mr H A Brown bought a Daimler motorcar and had it converted into an eight-seat wagonette for use on a service from Donnington to the market town of Wellington. This area would later become Telford New Town and local operators, including Browns, prosper accordingly. To reduce friction among themselves the village bus companies formed the Shropshire Omnibus Association which coordinated timetables according to a rota system and represented the operators in legal and licencing matters. The Association was also seen as a counter-balance to the bulk of Midland Red. In the early 1950s the RAF airfields at Hodnet, Shawbury and Ternhill were at their peak, bringing lucrative forces leave work to Shropshire coach firms, and Browns were an eager participant in this trade. Five Beadle-bodied SLC4/35s were ordered new from Sentinel and became the backbone of the company's fleet along with a sixth, which had previously been a demonstrator. In later years most were converted for one-man operation on the local services around Telford. Browns also acquired two STC4/40 service buses, both formerly demonstrators, one direct from Sentinel and the other from Warner of Tewkesbury who had in turn bought it second-hand from Maryland Luxury Coaches, London. The Browns Sentinels proved to be the longest lived of them all in regular revenue service, with some lasting as late as 1973. This longevity assured them a place in the preservation movement, and no fewer than five of them survived, although one has since been dismantled for spares. The company itself proved more vulnerable and sold its services to Midland Red in April 1978, ceasing to trade as a coach operator later in the same year.
Vehicles: GUJ 608 (STC4/40/30), HAW 302 (SLC4/35/54), HAW 303 (SLC4/35/59), HAW 373 (SLC4/35/22), HAW 374 (SLC4/35/33), HNT 49 (SLC4/35/63), HNT 101 (SLC4/35/23), JUJ 264 (STC4/40/16).

CAELLOI MOTORS - see JONES, Pwllheli.

R CAMPION, Clonmel, Tipperary, Republic of Ireland
This enterprise began in the mid-1930s, developing stage carriage services from

Above: Sentinels served with three companies called Bluebird and with two companies which used the trading name 'Princess Bus Service'. One of these was in the Republic of Ireland, the other was Duggins of Newcastle-under-Lyme, Staffordshire. Here is Duggins's STC6/44 **VRF 822**, delivered new in 1951, resting on The Ironmarket stand in Newcastle before departure on the service to Silverdale.

Below: Edwards of Llangeinor, Glamorgan, bought this former Ribble STC6/44, **DRN 349**, in October 1963 and kept it for just over two years. It retained its Ribble livery throughout and was used on works contract services. The precise location of this shot is unknown, but there appears to be a half-cab member of the Brewer, Caerau, fleet in the background.

Clonmel to Thurles, and to the county town of Tipperary, using the trading name Princess Bus Service. The Sentinel replaced a prewar Daimler COG5 single-decker in 1959 and survived until 1965 when it was sold to a Dublin private-hire firm. There are rumours that the vehicle survives.
Vehicle: GTH 576 (STC6/44/98).

CAMPLEJOHN BROTHERS, Darfield, West Yorkshire

The four Camplejohn Brothers were pioneer operators of motorbuses in their part of Yorkshire, buying a ten-seat Humber as early as 1907. A daily service from Thurnscoe to Barnsley was developed in competition with Yorkshire Traction and other independents, and in postwar years Camplejohn gained a reputation as a stylish and formidable adversary. Two Sentinel STC6/44s were acquired in 1952, one new and the other an ex-demonstrator. A further Sentinel with a Burlingham bus body came from Whieldon's Green Bus, of Rugeley, in March 1957. With the surviving brothers anxious to retire, a decision was made to sell the business to the Yorkshire Traction Company in January 1961. The Sentinels received YTC livery and blinds for continued operation in the Barnsley area.
Vehicles: HAW 577 (STC6/44/82) f/n 28, LWT 880 (STC6/44/89) f/n 29, 775 ERF (63012) f/n 33.

CASTLE MOTOR COMPANY - see DREW AND WREN, Canterbury.

CEIRIOG VALLEY TRANSPORT - see PHILLIPS, Glyn Ceiriog.

M S CHARLTON & SONS, Newbrough, Northumberland

The Charlton family opened a private-hire business in Newbrough in 1919 and in 1934 acquired a route from Hexham to Haydon Bridge from another local operator. Charlton also specialised in works contracts and operated extensive networks in connection with the construction of the military testing range at Spadeadam. In October 1958 the surviving services of Moffit, Acomb (qv) were acquired along with an STC4/40, and in January 1961 (shortly after the Sentinel's departure) the company changed its name to Mid-Tyne Transport Limited. This failed to impress its creditors and it entered receivership shortly thereafter although continuing to operate.
Vehicle: ETY 174 (STC4/40/69) f/n A5.

H A C CLAIREAUX, Layham, Suffolk

C J Partridge started a horse-drawn carrier service from Layham in the 19th century and in 1916 acquired his first motorbus. This was used on a market-day service from Layham to Ipswich operated as Partridge and Son, and this trading name was retained when the business passed to Mr G C Partridge's son-in-law, Mr Claireaux, in April 1956. Under Mr Claireaux's leadership the company began a gradual programme of expansion, purchasing its first double-decker in 1961 and beginning the renewal of its single-deck fleet by replacing petrol-powered vehicles with diesels. Two Sentinels were acquired in the early 1960s: an SLC4/35 coach which had run for three different Lancashire operators, and an STC4/40 bus which had started life with Wigmore in the Sheffield area before migrating to Gloucestershire. A third Sentinel, the famous Western National machine exhibited at the 1948 Commercial Motor Show and later used by P. and M. Coach Line, was subsequently purchased for spares use. It lingered until 1964 before following its active cousins to the scrapyard. **Vehicles**: HOD 57 (SB4/40/2 - for spares use only), JWW 316 (STC4/40/15), NLG 176 (SLC4/35/29).

CLYNNOG & TREVOR MOTOR COMPANY LTD, Trevor, Caernarvonshire

Clynnog and Trevor (the anglicised spelling was then current) operated a service between Caernarvon and Pwllheli via the villages in the company's title. This commenced shortly before the First World War and for most of the fifty years before deregulation had a regular two-hour headway, alternating with an almost identical service provided by Crosville. Despite this apparent co-ordination neither operator's timings appeared in the other's timetable. With underdog bravado C & T displayed route number 082 in clear imitation of the larger company's N82 service. The operator's solitary Sentinel, a former Ribble STC6/44, arrived in September 1963 and appears to have been used

Above: Henry Hulley, of Baslow in Derbyshire, is regarded by enthusiasts as one of Britain's outstanding bus operators, serving challenging terrain in all weathers with an interesting fleet of pre-owned vehicles. Hulley's first underfloor-engined bus was this STC4/40, **NDE 555**, which received fleet number **16**. New to Morrison, of Tenby, it arrived in the Peak District after a short spell with Bellis in North Wales.

Below: K.W. Services of Daventry ran stage carriage routes in the Northamptonshire/Oxfordshire border area. This STC4/40, **GRP 105**, was the preferred vehicle for five years until its sale to a Staffordshire operator in early 1957.

in service for less than a month before being placed in open storage at the depot. It was later used as an equipment shed before gradually rotting into the Welsh landscape.
Vehicle: DRN 348 (STC6/44/46).

CONNOR & GRAHAM LTD, *Easington, East Yorkshire*

R C Connor and J H Graham began a service from Hull to Kilnsea at the mouth of the Humber estuary in the late 1920s, operating via Ottringham, Patrington and Easington. Their initial equipment was a second-hand Thornycroft. By the time the brand-new Sentinel STC4/40 arrived in 1951 there were several secondary routes in operation, including services from Withernsea to Easington, Kilnsea and Spurn Point, and a variation on the Hull service which operated via the remote village of Sunk Island. In 1954 Mr Connor retired and was replaced by his partner's son, Mr T W Graham. The limited company was formed in April of the following year. Double-deckers were used on the main service to Hull at peak times, with the Sentinel covering most other timings until its withdrawal in 1960. Its replacement was a coach-bodied Leyland of identical vintage but - with a sliding central entrance - less suited to stage carriage work.
Vehicle: JWF 176 (STC4/40/27).

G COOPER & SON, *Oakengates, Shropshire*

By 1927 Mr G Cooper had three 14-seat Willys Overland buses in service on a route from Wellington to Wrockwardine Wood, site of the original garage. As with other Telford-area operators, Cooper participated in the Shropshire Omnibus Association rota. Half-cab Crossleys were favoured in the late 1940s, but in 1950 the company ordered two of the new STC4/40s from its near neighbours at Shrewsbury. It is likely that only one of these was actually delivered, although both were painted in full Cooper livery and titles. The Sentinel which was definitely used in service proved unpopular because of its engine problems and was returned to the manufacturer in May 1952 before resale to Delaine. Cooper soldiered on until 1973 when the business was engulfed by Midland Red.
Vehicles: GNT 961 (STC4/40/14), GUJ 457 (STC4/40/31 - probably cancelled before delivery).

CORVEDALE MOTOR COMPANY LTD, *Ludlow, Shropshire*

In March 1939 Mr E E Williams purchased a Ludlow-Bridgnorth route from Wye Valley Motors of Hereford along with three vehicles: a Reo, a Dennis Lancet and a Bedford WTB coach. These assets formed the basis of the new Corvedale company (it took its name from the river which flows through Ludlow), which immediately embarked upon a decade of expansion by acquisition. By 1950 Corvedale vehicles were running from Ludlow to Bridgnorth, Walsall, and Worcester, while local services were reaching most of the villages in southern Shropshire, at least on market days. In March 1951 the first of two STC4/40s was delivered; they were allocated to the prestigious long-distance routes to more populous areas. Corvedale had expanded too quickly and in May 1953 a cashflow crisis prompted the sale of the Bridgnorth, Walsall, and Worcester services to Midland Red. The Sentinels, which had proved troublesome, were no longer needed as the remaining weekday services to Cleobury North, Ditton Priors and Tenbury could barely support Bedford OBs, let alone 40-seat vehicles on expensive hire-purchase arrangements. One was returned to Sentinel, to be refurbished for Delaine, while the other went off on long-term hire to Chapple, of Raglan, briefly returning to Ludlow in 1957 before eventual sale to Mid-Wales Motorways. Corvedale was purchased by the Yeomans family, of Hereford, when Mr Williams retired in 1965, but was maintained as a separate business and in 1969 was resold to Whittle of Highley.
Vehicles: GUX 524 (STC4/40/25) f/n 30 and later 24, HAW 180 (STC4/40/68) f/n 29.

H E CRAIGGS COACHES LTD, *Amble, Northumberland*

Founded in 1921 by Mr W Craiggs, this operator developed a local service in Amble between Chevington Drift and Hadstone, later extended to the postwar Links Estate. The ex-Trimdon STC4/40 arrived in December 1960 and lasted for nearly three years before resale to Appleby, of Choppington (qv). In later years

Above: SLC4/35 **BEJ 190** is seen at the remote Pontrhydygroes depot of its owners, Lloyd-Jones Brothers, keeping company with Tilling-Stevens K6MA7 **ETH 949**. Lloyd-Jones operated infrequent stage services into the local market town of Aberystwyth and seemed to like obscure vehicle types.

Below: Llynfi Motor Services, of Maesteg, collected a trio of second-hand Sentinels in the mid-1950s. Two of them were standard STC6/44s, the third was entirely unique: **KUX 412** was an SLC6/30 demonstrator built as a joint venture with Newcastle Sentinel dealer K. & B. who specified an unusual dual-door service bus body manufactured by local company Associated Coach Builders. K. & B. thought the combination would sell well to County Durham/Northumberland independents, but no orders were forthcoming and it was sold off to Moffit of Acomb, still in dual-door configuration. It had lost its rear door some time before purchase by Llynfi.

the stage service was operated by bus-bodied Bedfords and Fords while the company expanded considerably by acquisition of nearby operators.
Vehicle: OUP 582 (STC4/40/83).

DAISY BUS SERVICE LTD, Broughton, Lincolnshire
Daisy operated services from Scunthorpe to the Humberside villages of Broughton and Brigg along with a seasonal route through those communities to Cleethorpes. Various aging service buses were the regular performers, but in the summer anything that moved was employed, including the company's solitary Sentinel coach. The Beadle-bodied SLC4/27, acquired from the Trimdon fleet, was owned for just over a year.
Vehicle: PPT 213 (4273).

DARTMOOR BUS COMPANY - see WOOLLEY & ENGLISH, Haccombe

DAVIES BROTHERS (PENCADER) LTD, Pencader, Carmarthenshire
D S and W J Davies started bus operations in 1926, initially replacing a service from Carmarthen to Lampeter abandoned by Daniel Jones. A basic two-hourly headway was established and traffic boosted by adding a feeder service from Llandysul which met the trunk route at Pencader. The company's only Sentinel, an STC6/44, was delivered in January 1952 and was withdrawn in July 1954, soon finding a new home down the road at Llynfi Motors (qv). It later became the only Sentinel known to have operated on stage services in the Republic of Ireland, with Campion of Clonmel (qv).
Vehicle: GTH 576 (STC6/44/98).

DELAINE COACHES LTD, Bourne, Lincolnshire
The Delaine-Smith family bought their first bus in 1919, a 14-seat Model T Ford, and began to develop a network of local services from Bourne to Essendine, Grantham, Peterborough, Spalding and Stamford. From the very early days the Peterborough route assumed prominence and was soon operating on an hourly headway. Double-deckers arrived in the postwar era, along with two Sentinel STC4/40s, which had previously been returned to the manufacturer by their original owners but performed well in the flatlands of Delaine's territory. The two buses remained in the fleet until 1958 when they were sold to local buyers, one passing to Morley, of Whittlesey, the other to Whippet, of Hilton (qv). Delaine continues in business as one of the country's most stylish and widely respected independent bus operators.
Vehicles: GNT 961 (STC4/40/14) f/n 36, HAW 180 (STC4/40/68) f/n 38.

ROBERT DICKSON JUNIOR LTD, Dundee, Angus
Primarily an operator of extended coach tours from Dundee, Edinburgh and Glasgow, Dickson provided a stage carriage service from Dundee to Fowlis Easter via Downfield, Muirhead and Liff. The Sentinel was bought for this service and when the stage carriage route was sold to J D McGibbon of Liff in 1953 and later to T D Alexander (Greyhound Coaches), of Arbroath, the bus became surplus to requirements and migrated south to a Cornish operator. Dickson's main touring business was sold to Wallace Arnold of Leeds in 1963.
Vehicle: AYJ 822 (STC4/40/12) f/n 3.

D F DREW & D E WREN, Canterbury, Kent
This partnership, a rare bastion of independent bus operation in the monopolised south-east, traded as the Castle Motor Company. The stage service from Canterbury to Chartham passed to the partnership in 1956, having previously been operated by Mr Drew as a sole proprietor. The Sentinel, a former demonstrator acquired from Whieldon in 1957, had already gone by the time the partnership was dissolved in 1961, replaced by a new Thames Trader with Duple Midland bodywork.
Vehicle: GNT 190 (STC4/40/4).

IRENE DUGGINS, Newcastle-under-Lyme, Staffordshire
Miss Irene Duggins's grandfather began services between Newcastle and Silverdale in 1923 with a Model T Ford, using the trading name Princess Bus Service. In 1951 Miss Duggins took delivery of a new Sentinel STC6/44 and when Potteries Motor Traction proposed the acquisition of her business later in

Above: Longstaff, of Ravensthorpe, operated a stage service from Mirfield to Dewsbury, deep in the heart of Yorkshire Woollen District country, and their two-tone blue livery made a pleasant change from the drab red of the larger operator. STC4/40 **OUP 579** had started its career with Trimdon Motor Services and had had three further owners before purchase by Longstaff. It ran for them from 1961 until its sale to Phillips of Shiptonthorpe in 1965.

Below: In the later Mid-Wales Motorways livery of dark blue and cream, this is STC4/40 **GUX 524** on the inspection ramp at the Mid-Wales Newtown depot. The vehicle had been delivered new to Corvedale, of Ludlow, and had also served with Chapple, of Raglan, before finding its way to Montgomeryshire. It was the only Mid-Wales Sentinel to survive the disastrous depot fire in July 1969, and remained in service until the following year when it was scrapped.

the same year they assigned a very low valuation to this vehicle. Miss Duggins declined to sell and in April 1954 acquired another Sentinel from Roberts, of Newport (qv), to emphasise her faith in the type.

For almost 15 years the two Sentinels maintained the Silverdale route and its extension to Park Site Estate, operated jointly with PMT who used the route number 103 on their timings. Miss Duggins became Mrs Belshaw in 1965 and eventually sold out to her joint operators in 1977.

Vehicles: ODE 280 (STC6/44/92) f/n 2, VRF 822 (STC6/44/88), f/n 1.

EDWARDS BROTHERS, Beddau, Glamorganshire

Edwards Brothers began operations on the Pontypridd to Llantrisant road in the 1920s and marketed their service as part of the Amalgamated Bus Service bus-owners' co-operative. Eventually the remaining partners in this venture were absorbed by the largest of their number, Bebb, of Llantwit Fardre. The Sentinel was acquired from Broadway Coaches (qv) and operated with Edwards for only two months before disappearing.

Vehicle: HAW 179 (STC4/40/77).

EDWARDS BROTHERS MOTORS, Crymmych, Pembrokeshire

Founded in 1925 by Benjamin and John Edwards and initially operated a service from Cardigan to Clynderwen, later extended to Narberth. In 1949 the company began seasonal services from Cardigan and Crymmych to Tenby, a valuable source of revenue in the summer months. The two Sentinels were purchased to cater for this new traffic, and were later joined by a third, purchased second-hand from Pritchard, of nearby Narberth. Benjamin Edwards died in 1947 and ten years later John Edwards retired, selling the business to Rees and Phillips (qv). As the garage at Crymmych was halfway between Cardigan and Tenby they chose to use Midway Motors as their new trading name.

Vehicles: NDE 689 (SLC4/35/57), NDE 799 (STC4/40/24), ODE 182 (STC6/44/90).

ENTERPRISE BUS COMPANY, Otterhampton, Somerset

This little-known independent operator, for many years owned by members of the Haybittel family, was the sole provider of stage-carriage services in a triangular area between the main coast road, the River Parrett, and the Bristol Channel, situated to the north-west of Bridgewater. Enterprise's vehicles operated infrequent daily services from this small market town to the villages of Combwich, Otterhampton, Stockland, Stogursey, Burton, and Shurton, while Wed/Sat market-day journeys provided additional service to Coulting and to Stolford on the coast. This latter village would later lie in the shadow of the Hinckley Point Nuclear Power Station.

The Enterprise fleet, usually consisting of half a dozen coaches and a couple of well-used half-cab service buses, entered its own nuclear age in March 1954 with the most uncharacteristic acquisition of a four-year old STC4/40 which lasted for just under three years on the Otterhampton run before moving to Gloucestershire.

Vehicle: JWW 316 (STC4/40/15).

GREEN BUS COMPANY - see WHIELDON, Rugeley

T G HARRIES, Prendergast, Pembrokeshire

Harries traded as PRENDERGAST MOTORS and was strictly a private-hire and excursion operator until 1951 when he acquired the Haverfordwest to Broad Haven service of J Griffiths and Son. The Sentinel was ordered for this service and kept until 1958 when negotiations began to sell the stage-carriage route to Western Welsh. The licence was transferred in August 1959 and Harries concentrated on coaching.

Vehicle: ODE 40 (STC4/40/71).

W L HEARD, Hartland, Devonshire

As a typical village coach operator, Heard's activities ranged across private hires, day excursions, schools contracts, and the once almost-obligatory stage-carriage service. In Heard's case this was a Monday/Wednesday/Friday route which wound through tiny villages from Welcombe to Hartland, itself barely more than a hamlet. On certain journeys connections to larger shopping venues were offered via Western National. The

Above: STC6/44 **YRF 733** had served with Green Bus, Riviera, and Trimdon Motor Services before going to Milson, of Coningsby, in Lincolnshire. It is seen here operating the market day service to Boston, looking resplendent in Milson's attractive livery of maroon, red and cream.

Below: Moffitt, of Acomb, ran services in the sparsely populated area of Northumberland between Hadrian's Wall and the Scottish border, and STC4/40 **ETY 174** must have been a major investment. The vehicle is seen in Newcastle-upon-Tyne and spent its entire working life in the north-east of England.

former Tor Bus STC4/40 arrived from Venner, of Witheridge, in 1957 and was used for a single summer season before disappearing. Twenty years later it was found as a hut at the Porton Down germ-warfare establishment in Wiltshire and is now in preservation.
Vehicle: LOD 974 (STC4/40/32).

HENRY HULLEY & SONS, Baslow, Derbyshire

The legendary Henry Hulley's first stage carriage service opened in 1921, operating from Chesterfield to Baslow where Hulley bought a house and adjacent land for vehicle parking. In the following year the route was extended from Baslow to Bakewell, and was later further extended to Youlgreave in the hills to the south. In 1925 service 2 began operating from Chesterfield via Baslow to Tideswell and additions in the 1930s resulted in further routes to Eyam, Grindleford and Hartington; all were prime destinations for summer ramblers and the annual Bakewell Show provided further revenue for the pioneering operator. Most of Hulley's vehicles during this era were brand-new Leylands or Maudslays. Postwar purchasing policy saw quality second-hand vehicles preferred, particularly AECs and Leylands with BET-style bus bodywork by Burlingham and Roe. The increasing impact of the private car on Hulley's revenue showed in vehicles of unusual pedigree in later years. Oddities were cheaper and Hulley's mechanics could make anything go. Baslow became a mecca for enthusiasts. Among the one-off purchases of the period was an STC4/40, acquired from a North Wales operator in 1959 but new to Morrison of Tenby. Despite the hilly local landscape it performed well and lasted for more than four years before being replaced by even more eccentric vehicles - a quartet of Midland Red's home-made single-deckers which nobody else had ever dared to operate. The Hulley family sold the business to their neighbours, Silver Service, of Matlock in 1978, but the Hulley name resurfaced in 1989 when the Baslow-based operations were sold to two former employees.
Vehicle: NDE 555 (STC4/40/79) f/n 16.

T H JONES & SON, Pwllheli, Caernarvonshire

Jones, operating as Caelloi Motors, began a weekday service from the coastal resort town of Pwllheli to various remote villages in the hills of the Lleyn peninsula in the late 1920s. In this chapel-ridden part of North Wales, Sunday services were never seen as a possibility, but Caelloi's services prospered on the other six days and settled down to provide a basic Pwllheli-Dinas-Rhosddu schedule employing one vehicle plus duplicates on market days. This operation was a minor part of Mr Jones's holdings which included several coaching firms across North Wales. The Sentinel had started life with Connor and Graham on the Humber estuary and then migrated westwards as far as it was possible to go to reach Caelloi. It arrived in Pwllheli in September 1960 and was replaced a few years later by a former Northern General Tiger Cub.
Vehicle: JWF 176 (STC4/40/27).

K.W. SERVICES, Daventry, Northamptonshire

This partnership was formed in 1932 to amalgamate the bus services of Messrs. Kingston and Welton, operating from Daventry via Northampton to Banbury. A daily service serving the three towns was slowly assembled despite the hostility of Midland Red and their adjacent area-agreement brethren. Timings were coordinated with those of another independent, Owen, of Upper Boddington (qv), and it came as no surprise when both operators tried Sentinels. K.W.'s machine arrived first in the form of an STC4/40 delivered in 1951 and this vehicle remained the company's workhorse until 1958 when a change in policy resulted in luxury coaches being used on the stage services. The company became Taylor & K.W. Coaches Ltd after a merger in the 1970s and in October 1980 the combined business was purchased by Geoff Amos Coaches, of Eydon. Amos had already acquired Owen some nine years previously. By 1983 the K.W. name had disappeared.
Vehicle: GRP 105 (STC4/40/72) f/n S1.
LEWIS MOTORS (FALMOUTH) - see *RIVIERA, Mylor Bridge*

LLOYD-JONES BROTHERS, Pontrhydygroes, Cardiganshire

This hilltop operator began a market-day stage service from Pontrhydfendigoid to

Above: This STC4/40, **GAY 50**, was delivered to Boyer, of Rothley, but did not pass to Midland Red, being sold a few weeks before the takeover. Its new owner was the Warwickshire independent, Monty Moreton, and it is seen here in Nuneaton bus station operating the local service to Gipsy Lane, in a sense opening a second front in its one-bus war against Midland Red.

Below: **HAW 180** had been new to the Ludlow operator Corvedale, and then passed to Delaine, of Bourne, before finding a third operator, Morley, of Whittlesey in Cambridgeshire. Morley's livery of red and grey suited the STC4/40 very well. The location is Peterborough bus station.

93

Aberystwyth in 1920 but the upper reaches of the route proved uneconomic and it was soon cut back to run from the garage instead. The Sentinel coach was delivered in April 1951, joining a varied fleet which ranged from Bedfords to Tilling-Stevens, and soon became the vehicle of choice for the run to Aberystwyth. It also ventured further afield with reported sightings at Blackpool, Llandudno and Wembley Stadium, before its sale some seven years later to an operator in distant Northumberland. The service to Aberystwyth ended in 1970, by then being operated by Bedfords.
Vehicle: BEJ 190 (SLC4/35/21).

LLYNFI MOTOR SERVICES LTD, *Maesteg, Glamorganshire*

W G Thomas began a service from Maesteg to Port Talbot in 1924, operating jointly with South Wales Transport. He also operated extensive contract services in connection with the massive Port Talbot steelworks, and schools services in the Maesteg area. The name of Llynfi Motor Services was adopted in the late 1920s and the limited company founded in the 1930s. Llynfi's first Sentinel, a former STC6/44 demonstrator, arrived at Maesteg in 1952 and was joined two years later by an identical machine originally delivered to Davies Brothers, of Pencader. A third vehicle was purchased in 1955, this one the SLC6/30 bus demonstrator with A.C.B. bodywork which had spent a few months with Cecil Moffit at Acomb before heading south. For several years the three Sentinels were the mainstays of Llynfi's fleet before being replaced in 1958-60 by Leylands.
Vehicles: GTH 576 (STC6/44/98) f/n 64, GUX 614 (STC6/44/95) f/n 63, KUX 412 (6307) f/n 65.

J J LONGSTAFF & SONS, *Ravensthorpe, West Yorkshire*

Longstaff began a service from Mirfield to Dewsbury via Knowle in 1928, using a second-hand Leyland PLSC Lion. More Leylands followed with the first double-decker, a Burlingham-bodied PD1, arriving in 1947. AECs were preferred in the 1950s, but the monotony was broken in November 1961 by the addition of a fifth-hand STC4/40. This machine had started its career with Trimdon, passed initially to a contractor, then to Gee and Harrison, of Whittington near Lichfield, who used it on contract services for British Railways among others, and then to Phillips of Glyn Ceiriog (qv) before arriving on the Mirfield run. After four years in service with Longstaff it was sold to another Phillips, this one the Phillips Coach Company, of Shiptonthorpe.
Vehicle: OUP 579 (STC4/40/73).

MAJESTIC MOTORS - see RICHARDSON, Thorne

MIDLAND RED - see BIRMINGHAM & MIDLAND MOTOR OMNIBUS CO. LTD, Smethwick

MID-WALES MOTORWAYS LTD, *Newtown, Montgomeryshire*

Mid-Wales Motorways was founded in 1937 to amalgamate the stage carriage services of six small operators in the Upper Severn Valley area of central Wales. Within a year, two more operators had joined the consortium, giving the company a virtual monopoly of services in the region. Further expansion came in 1936 with the acquisition of Worthen and District over the border in Shropshire. This brought important new routes from Four Crosses, Newtown and Welshpool to Shrewsbury, connecting these remote communities to mainline railway services. The company's headquarters building in Newtown became a source of some local pride as the almighty Crosville empire was held at bay. Mid-Wales's last profitable year was 1949 but the illusion persisted for a while, especially with a fleet of modern underfloor-engined Sentinels coming into service. Two of these were delivered new in 1950/1 and immediately assumed responsibility for the trunk services to Shrewsbury and the busy Newtown to Montgomery route. The Shrewsbury services were still well-enough patronised to justify double-deckers on busy days, but later in the decade two second-hand STC4/40s were acquired to reflect the lessening demand. The first came from Corvedale (qv) and the other was the former Cooper, of Oakengates, vehicle which had also seen service with Delaine and Whippet. In

Above: Morrison, of Tenby, bought STC4/40 **NDE 555** direct from the manufacturer and kept it in service for just over seven years. It became better known towards the end of its life when it ran for Henry Hulley in the Peak District.

Below: **HAW 179** was new to Smith's Eagle, of Trench, but they remained unimpressed and after just over a year the STC4/40 was sold to Nickolls, of Milford in neighbouring Staffordshire. The vehicle was the mainstay of that operator's solitary stage service for ten tears and is seen here at their Stafford terminus , ahead of a pre-war Midland Red FEDD double-decker.

1963 the company's financial instability became obvious to all when creditors had a receiver appointed and the original business went into liquidation. All was not lost, however, as Mid-Wales Motorways (1963) Limited emerged phoenix-like from the ashes. The new company had fewer vehicles (33 as opposed to 46), fewer routes, fewer personnel and fewer fixed assets, but it still had its flagship Sentinels along with a large number of Bedford OBs. On 19th July 1969 a disastrous fire destroyed the Newtown garage and thirteen vehicles, including three Sentinels. Unable to meet its commitments, Mid-Wales negotiated the sale of its key Shrewsbury services and concentrated on its local services in the Newtown area.

Vehicles: BEP 864 (STC4/40/16), CEP 147 (STC4/40/70), GNT 961 (STC4/40/14), GUX 524 (STC4/40/25).

MIDWAY MOTORS - see REES & PHILLIPS, Crymmych

H H MILSON LTD, Coningsby, Lincolnshire
Milson's prewar history was typical of that of many small village operators in Lincolnshire and elsewhere, with private-hire work and excursions balanced by some stage-carriage routes in connection with local market days. Milson operated to Sleaford on Monday, Boston on Wednesday and Saturday, and Horncastle (Saturday) while a service to Lincoln operated on Wednesday, Friday and Saturday. The development of a large Bomber Command airfield on their doorstep brought a welcome boost to Milson's revenues in the 1940s and 1950s and enabled them to maintain services at prewar levels when many operators were making drastic reductions. Expansion was also on the agenda, with the acquisition of Gosling, of Mareham-le-Fen, in 1960 with another assortment of market services. By September of that year demand had overwhelmed the Bedford OBs previously used on the Lincoln service and, to avoid duplication, the company acquired a fourth-hand Sentinel STC6/44. The vehicle had previously served with Whieldon's Green Bus in Staffordshire, Riviera in Cornwall and Trimdon in County Durham. Milson kept it for just over a year. The Milson business passed to Hogg, of Boston, in 1979.

Vehicle: YRF 733 (STC6/44/97).

C C MOFFIT, Acomb, Northumberland
Cecil Moffit began services from Newcastle to Hexham, Bellingham, and the higher Tyne valley in 1928 and had become the dominant operator in that part of Northumberland by 1939. The late 1940s were prosperous and funded a new Sentinel STC4/40 in 1951. This was followed in 1954 by acquisition of the SLC6/30 bus demonstrator with A.C.B. bodywork, which had been offered through the Newcastle Sentinel distributor, K and B Motors, but this vehicle had gone within a year. The STC4/40 was still in service when Mr Moffit sold out to M S Charlton (qv) in 1958.

Vehicles: ETY 174 (STC4/40/69) f/n 5 (also reported as C5), KUX 412 (6307).

MONTY MORETON LTD, Nuneaton, Warwickshire
One of a handful of independent operators in Warwickshire, Monty Moreton operated works-orientated services from Nuneaton to Hinckley and Wolvey along with more frequent local services from Nuneaton town centre to Gipsy Lane and the Caldwell Estate. In March 1959 the operator acquired an early model STC4/40 which had been delivered to Boyer, of Rothley. The vehicle was rostered for the local services, where it spent just over a year before replacement and sale for contract work in Ellesmere Port.

Vehicle: GAY 50 (STC4/40/3).

SAMUEL MORGAN LTD, Armthorpe, West Riding
Samuel Morgan started a service from Stainforth to Doncaster in August 1921 with a Model T Ford. In December 1930 the business was purchased by a rival operator on the route, Mr Richard Wilson, who began to use the trading name Blue Line for the Morgan service. This had been extended to run from Goole via Thorne and Stainforth to Doncaster, bringing it into competition with Richardson (Majestic Motors) who ran from Goole to Stainforth and to many of the coalmines in between. This competition was removed in 1953 when Morgan took control of Richardson's stage services along with the two Sentinels used to

Above: Good quality shots of the second SB4/40 prototype in service with P. & M. Coach Line proved hard to find, so we are particularly grateful to Geoff Mills for this excellent view of **HOD 57**, seen at the outer terminus awaiting the run back to Ipswich.

Below: The much-travelled STC4/40 **AYJ 822** ended its working life with Pooley, of Long Sutton, who painted it in this highly original livery for use round Fenland villages such as Gedney Drove End. It had previously served in Dundee and Cornwall.

operate them. Richard Wilson's people were deeply unimpressed with the STC4/40s which retained their worrisome 4SRH indirect injection engines. Richardson had apparently bought the two former demonstrators in as seen condition and thus they were ineligible for the free up-grade to 4SRH2 (4D) standard. After much overheating and many breakdowns whilst operating miners' works services the pair were withdrawn in 1955/8.
Vehicles: GNT 587 (STC4/40/20), GUJ 457 (STC4/40/31).

J R MORLEY & SONS LTD, Whittlesey, Cambridgeshire
Mr J R Morley began a service from Whittlesey to Peterborough in 1922, using two 14-seat Oldsmobiles. This route became the operator's main source of income for the next six decades despite competition from the Eastern Counties Omnibus Company and from fellow local independent Canhams, of Whittlesey. In later years the services of the three operators were coordinated to create a more regular headway between the two towns. The company's only Sentinel came with a good pedigree as Delaine had been operating it into Peterborough from the north for more than five years. Morley kept it for another five years, perhaps suggesting that STC4/40s were better suited to flat country. **Vehicle**: HAW 180 (STC4/40/68).

D J MORRISON, Tenby, Pembrokeshire
Morrison started his original service, from Tenby to Narberth and Whitland, in 1925. Expansion came in 1934 when a stage service from Tenby to Manorbier was acquired from Grey Garages whose coaching and other interests were unaffected. A new Sentinel STC4/40 joined the fleet in 1951 and became the regular performer on the two stage services until the Morrison business was sold to the neighbouring (but much larger) independent Silcox, of Pembroke Dock, in 1958.
Vehicle: NDE 555 (STC4/40/79).

T W MUNDY, Camborne, Cornwall
Mundy, who traded as Silver Queen, began his services from Camborne to Portreath and from Portreath to Redruth in the late 1920s. The early history of the business remains unrecorded but in the 1950s Mr Mundy attracted the attentions of bus enthusiasts by operating such rarities as a Saro-bodied Commer Avenger service bus (the only other known example went to Mid-Wales Motorways) and a Sentinel STC4/40 with a Dundee registration. This was the former Dickson machine, although how it came to be sold in Cornwall is a mystery. Mundy used the vehicle from 1953 until the end of 1956 when it was sold for further service with Pooley, of Long Sutton (qv). The Silver Queen name continued until 1965 when the business was absorbed by Grenville Motors, which later passed to Western National.
Vehicle: AYJ 822 (STC4/40/12).

H NICKOLLS & SON, Milford, Staffordshire
Nickolls began their Stafford to Hixon via Great Haywood service in the mid-1920s, exploiting the boundary zone between adjacent BET companies Midland Red and PMT. Essentially a one-bus operation, it operated to an approximately hourly headway on weekdays with no Sunday service. The Sentinel came second-hand from Smiths, of Trench (qv), who kept it for little more than a year. Nickolls kept it for ten, replacing it with a Bedford/Plaxton Conway bus in 1962 when the STC4/40 was sold to Sergent of Wrinehill (qv). The Plaxton Conway was still the service bus in June 1966 when Nickolls sold out to Greatrex, of Stafford. They swiftly replaced it with a Ford R192 more suited to driver-only operation.
Vehicle: HAW 179 (STC4/40/77).

G T OWEN & SON LTD, Upper Boddington, Northamptonshire
Owen started a service between Upper Boddington and Banbury via Eydon in the 1920s and this eventually grew to operate on six days per week. All other services were essentially market-day journeys and ran to Northampton (Wednesday and Saturday), Rugby (Monday) and Leamington (Friday). Many of these services were loosely coordinated with those of another local independent, KW Services, of Daventry (qv), and when KW bought a new Sentinel STC4/40 in July 1951 Owen took a keen interest in the vehicle's performance. When the company placed an order it was for the larger STC6/44, and the vehicle materialised in August 1952 as

Above: Possibly the most famous STC4/40 of them all, Potter of Haytor's **LOD 974**, resplendent in their magnificent Tor Bus livery of maroon and red with signwritten route details above the side windows. Long presumed to have been scrapped it was rediscovered at a military surplus auction and has been restored to roadworthy condition by a preservation group.

Below: This STC6/44 is also preserved (the only confirmed survivor of the type), but is seen here when in service with Rees and Phillips, of Crymmych. The partnership operated as Midway Motors and acquired the earlier business of Edwards Brothers Motors along with this vehicle, **ODE 182**. It spent its entire working life at Crymmych, wearing a variety of liveries, all of them mainly blue, until being retired and used as a storage shed at the depot. A later shot in this book shows it as it looks today.

NNN 998 - registered for, but never delivered to, Leon of Finningley. It maintained the trunk route to Banbury for five years before being sold to Trimdon Motor Services. Owen continued until 1971 when it was taken over by Geoff Amos Coaches of Eydon.
Vehicle: NNN 998 (STC6/44/94).

P. & M. COACH LINE LTD, Ipswich, Suffolk
This company was formed in 1939 by an amalgamation of Primrose Coaches and Marguerite Coaches. Postwar they were noted for oddities in the fleet, including a TD1 Titan and an AEC Regent which were cut down to single-deck and given new coach interiors. In 1957, a Plaxton-bodied Sentinel SLC6/30 coach was acquired from Blue Bird Garages, of Hull, which remained in the fleet for seven years. In the middle of that period the company's stage carriage service, from Ipswich to Otley, was briefly graced by the former Western National Sentinel-Beadle, HOD 57, which arrived in Ipswich after a two-year stint with Sheriff (Star Service), in Gainsborough. It lasted for another two years with P & M before being sold to Claireaux for use as a source of spares. The P & M name endured until December 1968 when the business was sold to Progressive, of Cambridge, who soon placed it into liquidation. The stage service passed to Bickers of Coddenham.
Vehicles: HOD 57 (SB4/40/2) f/n 52, RAT 645 (63016) f/n 51.

PAMELA COACHES - see POOLEY, Long Sutton

PARTRIDGE & SON - see CLAIREAUX, Layham

L G PHILLIPS, Glyn Ceiriog, Denbighshire
Phillips, who sometimes traded as Ceiriog Valley Transport, operated a weekday stage carriage service from Llanarmon to Oswestry via Glyn Ceiriog and Bronygarth. This route was jointly operated with Vagg, of Knockin Heath on the English side of the border. The Sentinel, a former Trimdon STC4/40, arrived in June 1961 having been purchased from the Everall dealership in Wolverhampton. After two months in the gruellingly steep terrain of Denbighshire it was returned to Everall and Phillips took a Bedford instead.
Vehicle: OUP 579 (STC4/40/73).

PIONEER (Carmarthenshire) - see WILLIAMS, Laugharne

PIONEER (Pembrokeshire) - see ROBERTS, Newport

H POOLEY (HOLBEACH) LTD, Long Sutton, Lincolnshire
Pooley, previously a private-hire operator, became involved in stage carriage services through the acquisition of J R Flatt and Sons, of Long Sutton, in 1956. The purchase brought weekday services from Long Sutton to Wisbech, a Saturday only route from Gedney Drove End, in the marshlands of The Wash, to Wisbech, and market day services to Boston and Kings Lynn. For several years the business operated as Pamela Coaches, in honour of the proprietor's then current wife, and the Sentinel (which arrived in 1957 from Silver Queen) carried these titles until the situation changed. In 1958 an SLC4/35 was acquired for spares. The business ceased trading in June 1970 and the services passed to Carnell, but this was seven years after the demise of the Sentinels.
Vehicles: AYJ 822 (STC4/40/12), NTB 955 (SLC4/35/56).

J POTTER & SONS LTD, Haytor, Devonshire
Potter began a service from Liverton to Newton Abbot in 1921, and this was gradually extended, a village at a time, until it reached Widecombe in 1927. This slow process of route expansion reflected the late arrival of navigable roads on Dartmoor rather than any laziness on the part of the operator. The trading name was Tor Bus, which became well known to thousands of tourists and ramblers over the years, both for its reliable and relatively frequent services, and for the stylish colour scheme and well-groomed appearance of its vehicles. At busy times (such as the famous Widecombe Horse Fair) visitors would often be welcomed by the incongruous sight of Devon General vehicles bearing stickers proudly announcing that they were on hire to Tor Bus. The Sentinel was delivered in 1950 and became an instant celebrity by virtue of its modern appearance compared to most Dartmoor

Above: Rees & Williams of Tycroes bought this SLC6/30 with Whitson 'STC6 Lookalike' bodywork in the summer of 1954 and registered it **KBX 630**. Note the non-standard grille on the lower front panel, and the application of the side trim which makes even R. & W.'s attractive burgundy, red and white livery look strange. These refinements were peculiar to the dual-purpose version of the Whitson bus body and were a not entirely successful attempt to give the vehicles a more coach-like appearance.

Below: Ribble's STC6/44 fleet was originally based at Carlisle, but the vehicles' first-rate performance on hills soon resulted in many of them being transferred southwards to depots in the Lake District. **DRN 353** ended up at Penrith and is seen here operating service 623 to the village of Renwick.

service buses. Despite the presence of several fairly steep climbs on the Tor Bus route it performed well and shared the year-round service with an equally rare Metalcraft-bodied AEC Regal IV which carried three more passengers but weighed two tons more. The Sentinel's regular driver (now sadly deceased) recalled one Horse Fair journey on which approximately ninety passengers were crammed into the STC4/40 until the distant prospect of a police car resulted in a sudden stop to unload through the rear emergency exit. This stalwart of the moor was eventually sold in late 1956, replaced for the following summer season by a Burlingham-bodied AEC Reliance. The Sentinel passed via schools service operator Venner, of Witheridge, to Heard, of Hartland (qv), and then (after a long period presumed lost) into the hands of preservationists in 1980. It is currently roadworthy and looks resplendent in its version of the Tor Bus livery.
Vehicle: LOD 974 (STC4/40/32).

PRENDERGAST MOTORS - see HARRIES, Prendergast

PRINCESS BUS SERVICE (Ireland) - see CAMPION, Clonmel

PRINCESS BUS SERVICE (Staffordshire) - see DUGGINS, Newcastle-under-Lyme

W S REES & T D PHILLIPS, Crymmych, Pembrokeshire
Messrs Rees and Phillips purchased the long-established business of Edwards Brothers Motors (qv) in 1957 and began trading on the former EBM routes under the name MIDWAY MOTORS. It seems that EBM's STC4/40 was not included in the deal, but their STC6/44 was and duly appeared with Midway fleetnames. In 1968 Phillips withdrew from the partnership and was replaced by Mr W Rees, with father and son continuing to operate as Midway Motors. The routes changed little over the years, being essentially a Cardigan to Narberth trunk service reinforced in the summer months by services from Cardigan and Crymmych to Tenby. After withdrawal from daily service the STC6/44 was parked alongside the depot for more than a decade and survived long enough to be rescued by preservationists. It is currently being rebuilt in West Yorkshire.
Vehicle: ODE 182 (STC6/44/90).

REES & WILLIAMS LTD, Tycroes, Carmarthenshire
This business was founded in 1920 as a partnership of D J Rees, Lewis Rees and C B Williams, becoming a limited company in 1926. Its primary stage services were from Llandeilo to Swansea and from Llandeilo to Llanelli, both operating via Ammanford and jointly operated with South Wales Transport. Despite being a non-standard type in every respect (chassis/engine/body) the Sentinel served on the Llandeilo routes for a full twelve years before resale for further use by two small local operators.
Vehicle: KBX 630 (63019).

RELIANCE COACHES - see SIMMONS, Great Gonerby

RIBBLE MOTOR SERVICES LTD, Preston, Lancashire
Sentinel's leading customer was one of the largest and best-known bus companies in the British Isles and at the time of its order for STC types was operating more than 1,100 vehicles on a vast network of services, which stretched from the Solway Firth and Hadrian's Wall to Liverpool and Manchester in the south. More than a quarter of Ribble's vehicles were single-decker service buses and most were scheduled for replacement in the period 1950-5. If only half of these orders had gone to Sentinel it would have equalled the company's entire production run for other customers, but it was not to be. Ribble was impressed with its Sentinels, but the problems with the Ricardo engine had destroyed the newcomer's lead and once Leyland were back in the game the prospect of further triumphs in Preston quickly evaporated. Another factor in Ribble's return to the Leyland fold was undoubtedly the application of a stricter buying policy within the BET Group. Neighbouring company North Western, frustrated by Bristol's removal from the free market, had conspired with lorry-manufacturer Atkinson to produce a tailor-made, Gardner-powered, underfloor-engined single-decker and had wanted to order a large

Above: Richardson, of Thorne in the West Riding, traded as Majestic Motors and operated a frequent service from Goole to Stainforth. The final workhorses on this route were two STC4/40s, one of which, **GUJ 457**, is seen in Goole. Originally intended for Cooper, of Oakengates, this vehicle became a demonstrator instead and was then sold to Richardson as seen, complete with unmodified 4SRH engine. This led to its demise after the Majestic business was bought out by Samuel Morgan who had no time for such oddities.

Below: **YRF 734** was one of a quartet of Green Bus STC6/44s sold to Riviera in Cornwall in 1957. The board in the route number box declaring it to be a Lewis vehicle is misleading: each vehicle contained both Lewis and Riviera boards to fit this aperture and they were changed around according to the route being operated. Lewis, a wholly-owned subsidiary of Riviera, held the licence for a service from Falmouth to Gyllyngvase Beach.

number but this was frustrated by Group policy, which focussed on economies of scale rather than the operational preferences of subsidiaries. Although this was only given written expression in 1952 (and resulted in the resignation of North Western's Chief Engineer), it was rumoured that Ribble had also been brought into line, if only by means of subtle comment and metaphorical tutting noises.

After brief periods of testing on service 109 from Preston to Leyland and Chorley the Sentinels were sent into exile in Carlisle, with the four-cylinder variants largely confined to local services and those along the flattish roads of the Solway Firth, while the six-cylinder versions were used on the more challenging routes into the hills of the Lake District and Westmorland. Their time with Ribble was uneventful with the exception of an incident at Bowness-on-Solway on the evening of Wednesday, 17th October 1962. STC4/40 fleet number 281 (CRN 214) was passing through the village with the driver and three passengers on board when the engine started to race before catching fire. The driver evacuated the vehicle and then made an attempt to drive the vehicle out of the village, but the clutch burned out and the bus came to a halt across the road from Ribble's Bowness out-station where he was forced to abandon it as it was consumed by flames. It appears that the engine's tendency to overheat could still be a problem after twelve years in service with a major operator.

Until the summer of 1954 all twenty vehicles were based at Carlisle depot, the

DEPOT ALLOCATIONS OF RIBBLE SENTINELS

F/N	NEW	3/54	8/54	12/56	10/58	1/59	5/61	6/62	3/63	7/63	SOLD	Notes
278	5/49	C	C	C	C	C	C	C	C	C*	8/63	1
279	1/50	C	C	C	C	C	C	C	C	F*	8/63	2
280	5/50	C	C	C	C	C	C	C	C	C*	8/63	
281	5/50	C	C	C	C	C	C	C	-	-	-	3
282	5/50	C	C	C	C	C	C	C	C	-	5/63	2
283	7/50	C	C	C	C	C	C	C	C	-	4/63	2
284	1/51	C	C	P	P	P	P	P	P	P	7/63	2
285	1/51	C	C	C	C	C	U	U	C	C*	8/63	
286	1/51	C	C	C	C	C	U	U	U	U	7/63	
287	1/51	C	C	C	C	C	U	U	U	U	7/63	
288	1/51	C	C	C	C	C	C	A	A	A*	9/63	4
289	1/51	C	C	P	P	P	P	P	U	U*	7/63	
290	1/51	C	C	C	C	C	C	K	K	K	7/63	5
291	3/51	C	C	C	P	P	P	P	P	P*	8/63	
292	3/51	C	C	C	C	P	P	P	U	U*	7/63	
293	3/51	C	C	C	C	P	P	P	P	P	7/63	
294	3/51	C	C	P	P	P	P	P	U	U	7/63	
295	4/51	C	P	P	P	P	P	P	U	U*	7/63	
296	5/51	C	P	P	P	P	P	P	P	P	7/63	
297	5/51	C	P	C	P	P	P	P	P	P	7/63	

N.B. Fleet numbers 278-83 were delivered as 2722-7. See individual vehicle histories for further information. **A** = Ambleside; **C** = Carlisle; **F** = Preston; **K** = Kendal; **P** = Penrith; **U** = Ulverston. An asterisk * indicates a vehicle delicensed and stored.

Notes:- 1. Delivered to Preston; at Chorley by late 1950 and then Carlisle by 1951. **2.** Delivered to Preston; at Carlisle by 1951. **3.** Delivered to Carlisle; at Preston by 7/50 and then Carlisle again by 1951. Destroyed by fire at Bowness-on-Solway 17/10/62 and scrapped 11/62. **4.** Transferred to Ambleside by 11/61. Ribble's last Sentinel. **5.** Transferred to Kendal by 11/61.

Above: Roberts, of Newport (Pembrokeshire), took delivery of this STC4/40, **NDE 620**, in 1951 and kept it for eight years. It then moved on to Martin, of Weaverham in Cheshire, and from there went to Scotland before a return to England for further use as a mobile shop.

Below: Former Ribble STC6/44, **DRN 347**, is seen at the premises of its new owner, Rossmore, of Sandbanks in Dorset. Its career on the south coast was brief and given the vintage character of most of Rossmore's fleet (note vehicle to the left of the Sentinel) it may well have been too complicated for their tastes. Rossmore had bought a second STC6/44 to use as a source of spares, so this was an expensive experiment.

monopoly being broken by the transfer of three STC6/44s (295-7) to Penrith where they frequently ran over the high mountain passes to Kendal and Windermere. Their performance compared to Leyland types resulted in a permanent Sentinel presence at Penrith until the final withdrawal. Ulverston depot received its first STC6/44s in 1960 when Nos 285-7 were transferred in from Carlisle. By the summer of 1962 there were single examples operating from both Kendal and Ambleside garages. The STC4/40s were in less demand and remained at Carlisle throughout.

The entire batch (with the exception of the Bowness casualty) was withdrawn in 1963 and sold to Cowley, a vehicle dealer with yards at Salford and Pennington in Lancashire and at Dunchurch in Warwickshire. None of the STC4/40s saw further PSV usage, but several of the 6-cylinder versions found new operators, if only for comparatively short periods. None survived into preservation, a major oversight since one of the STC6/44s could still have been rescued from its Welsh resting place as late as 1972 - well into the preservationist era. Although there were only twenty of them in a fleet of more than a thousand Leylands, they were of greater historical significance than most preserved Ribble vehicles of that marque. It seems remarkable that of the nine Sentinel PSVs in preservation none is a Ribble vehicle. Ribble itself was dismembered over the years that followed, with the northern third of the company's area passing to fellow-Stagecoach subsidiary Cumberland Motor Services and the southern third being established as a separate company before privatisation. The remainder survived until the very end of the twentieth century when Stagecoach decided to sell the eastern half to Blazefield and restyle the rump (principally Preston and the Fylde coast) as Stagecoach in Lancashire, though the legal lettering still says Ribble.

Vehicles: CRN 211 (SB4/40/6) f/n 2722 then f/n 278, CRN 212-6 (STC4/40/7-STC4/40/11) f/ns 2723-7 then f/ns 279-83, DRN 341-54 (STC6/44/39-STC6/44/52) f/ns 284-97.

F RICHARDSON, Thorne, West Yorkshire
This business, which traded as Majestic Motors, began in 1929 as a partnership of Messrs Richardson and Hopley, later acquiring another local operator, Bradley, of Goole. The company's major source of revenue was a stage service from Goole to Thorne and Stainforth, but there were also many special workings to coalmines, such as Moorends, along the route. The Sentinels, both former demonstrators, were acquired at a bargain price in as seen condition and neither had been converted to direct injection. It is believed that problems with the vehicles served as a spur to Richardson's decision to withdraw from stage carriage work in 1953. The business, including the Sentinels, was sold to Morgan, of Armthorpe (qv. Mr Richardson continued as a coach operator, still using the Majestic Motors name.

Vehicles: GNT 587 (STC4/40/20), GUJ 457 (STC4/40/31).

RIVIERA SERVICES LTD, Mylor Bridge, Cornwall
The Hearle family began operations from Mylor Bridge in the 1920s, and gained a licence to operate a stage carriage service from there to the nearby towns of Penryn and Falmouth. The Riviera name was used and was later adapted as the title of a limited company. In 1957 the old-established business of Lewis Motors (Falmouth) Limited was acquired along with excursion licences and a seasonal stage service from Falmouth to Gyllyngvase Beach. The Lewis concern was kept in operation as a subsidiary although its vehicles were painted thereafter in an identical livery to those of Riviera. Also in 1957 a decision was taken to modernise the rather ancient fleets of both companies and four Sentinel STC6/44s were acquired from Whieldon's Green Bus, of Rugeley. The first of these, a former Sentinel demonstrator, was licenced to Lewis and spent most of its working life on the Beach service, while the other three were licensed to Riviera for the Mylor Bridge run. In service the Sentinels proved so reliable compared to their antique predecessors that one of the four vehicles (purchased as a reserve) was not needed and passed to Trimdon within a year. The last of the remaining three continued in service until 1965. Riviera Services continued until 1970 when the Hearle family sold the business to Grenville Motors, the rapidly expanding independent based at Troon, near Camborne. Grenville itself was taken over by

Above: The first SB4/40 prototype, **EUJ 792**, seen in service with Salopia Saloon Coaches. The location of the shot is given on the reverse of the photograph as Shrewsbury, but is believed to be in Whitchurch bus station at the other end of Salopia's main line service.

Below: Simmons, of Great Gonerby in Lincolnshire, traded as Reliance Coaches and operated several important local services in the Grantham area. In all they took three Sentinels, and this is the first, STC6/44 **GCT 181**. The location is Grantham bus station and the vehicle is still in its original two-tone blue livery. Along with the rest of the Simmons service bus fleet it was later repainted red and cream.

Western National shortly after deregulation of the industry.
Vehicles: HUJ 619 (STC6/44/81 - licensed to Lewis), YRF 732 (STC6/44/93), YRF 733 (STC6/44/97), YRF 734 (STC6/44/99).

H ROBERTS & SON, Newport, Pembrokeshire
Mr H Roberts started a timetabled service from Newport to Fishguard in 1918 using a five-seat saloon car. In 1921 the route, by then operated with a bus, was extended to run from Cardigan to Fishguard and Mr Roberts began to use the trading name Pioneer. From 1929 the service was jointly operated with the Great Western Railway, and later (in their stead) with Western Welsh. The first Sentinel, an STC4/40, arrived in July 1951 and became the regular vehicle on the coastal service. It seems to have performed well as an order was placed for an STC6/44 to be delivered in 1952. Strangely, this latter machine was kept in the fleet for only two years before sale to Duggins, of Newcastle-under-Lyme (qv), whereas the four-cylinder vehicle remained in use until 1959. The Roberts business continued until 1976 when it was absorbed by an independent neighbour, Richards Brothers, of Moylgrove.
Vehicles: NDE 620 (STC4/40/38), ODE 280 (STC6/44/92).

ROSSMORE BUS COMPANY LTD,
Sandbanks, Dorset
Local people in Poole used to refer to Rossmore's bus route as running from Heavenly Bottom to Monkey's Hump, which gives some idea of the area's topography. In terms the licencing authorities would understand, it ran from Albert Road, via Rossmore, to the Trinidad Estate, and despite its diminutive mileage did very well because of the gradient involved. In the summer season double-deckers were often required, and a succession of interesting older vehicles were to be found on the service. In November 1963 Rossmore acquired two former Ribble STC6/44s, but only one of these appears to have run in service with the second intended as a source of spares. However, there seem to have been problems as the active vehicle was withdrawn after only three months in use and subsequently allowed to become derelict at the depot, while the second machine disappeared from view and may never have arrived in Dorset.
Vehicles: DRN 347 (STC6/44/45), DRN 351 (STC6/44/49 - never operated).

SALOPIA SALOON COACHES LTD,
Whitchurch, Shropshire
In 1926 J R Richards and Sons opened for business in Whitchurch with a single Thornycroft coach. The operation grew steadily, developing both an extensive tours programme and a network of local bus services including a trunk route from Whitchurch to Shrewsbury via Wem. Other weekday services ran from Whitchurch to Market Drayton (via two routes), to Prees Heath, and to Wem (via a different route from that of the Shrewsbury service). In addition the company operated a number of market-day services, one of which crossed the county boundary to terminate at Nantwich, in Cheshire. In 1938 the business became Salopia Saloon Coaches Limited, formalising a title already used for marketing purposes. In postwar days the company became famous for its Foden/Whitson observation coaches and for the fact that it operated the original Sentinel-Beadle diesel bus, EUJ 792, on its local services. The Sentinel arrived at Whitchurch in March 1949 and spent most of the next twelve years on the Shrewsbury service before being sold in 1961 for conversion into a mobile shop. It is unfortunate that this vehicle, the prototype of Sentinel's pioneering design, was not preserved. Salopia itself went through several different owners before absorption by the Shearings empire and the gradual loss of its local identity.
Vehicle: EUJ 792 (SB4/40/1) f/n 60.

SARGEANT BROTHERS, Kington,
Herefordshire
By 1931 Mr C T Sargeant was operating stage carriage services from Kington to Builth Wells and Hay-on-Wye. Further expansion on the Welsh side of the border resulted in the establishment of two new limited companies in 1950, one based in Kington, the other in Builth Wells. In 1955 the Welsh company was sold while the Herefordshire services passed to a new partnership of A M and K Sargeant, trading as Sargeant Brothers. The operator's single Sentinel, a Beadle-bodied SLC4/35,

Above: Only two SLC6/30s were equipped with Whitson's dual-purpose variant of the STC6 body, KBX 630 *(see earlier picture)*, and this one which eventually became **SDF 17** with Warners, of Tewkesbury, after a spell as a Whitson demonstrator. In this shot it still wears the Warner livery of two-tone green but is operating for Talbott (Barry's Coaches), of Moreton-in-the-Marsh.

Below: **ODE 40** was delivered new to Harries, of Prendergast, but sold when that operator's stage services were acquired by Western Welsh. Its new owner, Trimdon Motor Services, had failed to repaint it by the time of this shot taken on the Durham service. Because of a change in policy the vehicle was sold after less than two years and eventually became a mobile shop.

arrived second-hand from Warner, of Tewkesbury, in May 1959 and saw regular use on market-day runs around the Herefordshire countryside. It lasted for just over a year before resale to a Nottinghamshire private-hire firm.
Vehicle: KDG 853 (SLC4/35/26).

C A R SERGENT, Wrinehill, Staffordshire
The village of Wrinehill, on the main road from the Potteries to Nantwich, is a quarter of a mile inside Staffordshire but has always had a Cheshire postal address as its mail travels via Nantwich. The village coach operator has also traditionally looked in both directions, as the bulk of its contract works services have been operated to coalmines and other industrial sites in Staffordshire, and its only stage carriage service headed straight for the county boundary and had 95% of its mileage in Cheshire. The Thursday and Saturday service from Wrinehill to Nantwich began in the 1930s and for 15 years after the war was operated by a bonneted Commer. This era came to an end in November 1962 when Sergent acquired a Sentinel STC4/40 for use on the stage service and on schools runs. This vehicle lasted until early 1964 when it was replaced by another Sentinel, this one a Beadle-bodied coach. By a bizarre coincidence this latter machine had once operated for the similarly-named Sargeant Brothers, causing some confusion to historians of the type. It survived until August 1964 and shortly thereafter the service to Nantwich was discontinued.
Vehicles: HAW 179 (STC4/40/77), KDG 853 (SLC4/35/26).

SHERIFF & SON, Gainsborough, Lincolnshire
For many years Sheriff operated a frequent local service in Gainsborough, running daily from Lea Village to Morton via the town centre. There was also a market-day run on Tuesdays from Gainsborough to East Stockwith, and both of these routes were marketed under the name Star Service. Sheriff's only Sentinel was the former Western National vehicle, which came to Gainsborough in 1958 and spent more than a year on the town service before passing southwards to P. & M. Coach Line in Ipswich. The Sheriff business was taken over by Eaglen (Eagre Coaches), also of Gainsborough, by which time the town service was being operated by Bedford VAMs.
Vehicle: HOD 57 (SB4/40/2).

SILVER QUEEN - see MUNDY, Camborne

W J SIMMONS & COMPANY, Great Gonerby, Lincolnshire
Wilfred Joseph Simmons, the son of a local taxi operator, bought a 14-seat Chevrolet bus in 1924 and put it to work between Great Gonerby and Grantham. To make fuller use of the vehicle, a second service from Grantham to Barrowby soon followed. A seasonal express service from the Grantham area to Skegness was another early development, and during this period the fleet began to use the trading name Reliance Coaches. Further expansion resulted in new services from Grantham to Bourne, Corby Glen, and Ropsley, establishing the network which survived through to deregulation with the exception of the Thursday-only service to Bourne which was discontinued in 1957. The first of Simmons's three Sentinels, an STC6/44 originally earmarked for Leon of Finningley but cancelled before delivery, arrived in June 1952, An externally identical machine was delivered in July of the following year, but this was actually one of the SLC6/30s with bodywork assembled by Whitson from Sentinel/Metal Industries components. This led to 1955's delivery, a magnificent SLC6/30 coach with luxurious Whitson Grand Prix bodywork. One-man-operation was introduced in 1962 and the surviving Sentinel bus (GCT 181) was adapted to this purpose. In the same year a new service from Grantham to the Earlsfield Estate began and was notable in being jointly operated with the Lincolnshire Road Car Company who had previously treated the Reliance fleet as if they were pirates operating in a sea of Tilling Green. The last of the Sentinel fleet was scrapped at the depot in June 1965. By this time the first of the trio had already been converted into a mobile church but enthusiasts had worshipped in Sentinels for years.
Vehicles: GCT 181 (STC6/44/80), HCT 618 (6308), JTL 469 (63020).

T G SMITH, Trench, Shropshire
By 1930 Smith was operating a Willowbrook-

Above: The 1953 STC6/44 demonstrator, JNT 763, was also acquired by Trimdon. Reregistered as **OUP 578**, it was repainted into this non-standard cream livery with a blue stripe along the coving panels, virtually the reverse of normal TMS practice at the time. After six years in service with Trimdon it was sold to Baddeley Brothers, of Holmfirth, as shown in an earlier photograph.

Below: The Warner two-tone green livery again, this time on Beadle-bodied SLC4/35 coach **KDG 853**, still in service with the Tewkesbury operator. Warners were quite enthusiastic about Sentinels and bought several second-hand examples. KDG 853 later served with operators in Herefordshire, Nottinghamshire and Staffordshire, before returning to Gloucestershire to end its days with Williams in the county town.

bodied Bean from his premises at Trench to Wellington, and soon became a member of the Shropshire Omnibus Association and thus a participant in the famous Telford rotas. In 1950 additional rota services were acquired with the business of Bircher Coaches and at around the same time the trading name of Smiths Eagle came into use. The operator's only Sentinel, a new STC4/40, arrived in April 1951 and was put to work on the rotas in Smith's green and primrose livery alongside the identical (but brown and orange) machine of Cooper, Oakengates (qv). Unlike their Telford neighbours at Browns, of Donnington Wood, both Cooper and Smith were profouindly unhappy with their Sentinels and disposed of them quickly (at a time when Browns were making a marketing slogan out of their 'locally built buses'). Smiths Eagle disposed of theirs after only 17 months, selling it to Staffordshire independent Nickolls, of Milford, who kept it for ten years with no apparent dissatisfaction though operating in very similar terrain to Smith's.

Vehicle: HAW 179 (STC4/40/77).

STAR SERVICE - see SHERIFF AND SON, Gainsborough

R B TALBOTT, Moreton-in-the-Marsh, Gloucestershire
Talbott operated as Barry's Coaches and provided market-day services from its hometown to Banbury, Chipping Norton, Evesham and Stratford-upon-Avon. The fleet was always a varied one and in 1957 a second-hand STC4/40 was purchased from Enterprise, of Otterhampton (qv), for use on the stage-carriage services and on local schools contracts. This lasted for two years before disposal but Mr Talbott appears to have developed a taste for the breed. In January 1960 the STC4/40 was replaced by an SLC6/30 with Whitson bus bodywork acquired from Warner, of Tewkesbury, and this continued in service until 1966. Meanwhile, in November 1960, Talbott had bought an SLC6/41 coach with Plaxton Venturer bodywork, also from Warners, but this had been traded in to Everalls within weeks of its arrival at Moreton.

Vehicles: JWW 316 (STC4/40/15), LDF 296 (SLC6/41/101), SDF 17 (63017).

TERRIER COACHES - see APPLEBY, Choppington

TRIMDON MOTOR SERVICES LTD, Trimdon Grange, County Durham
Many of the small bus companies which provided stage carriage services in County Durham were founded by coalminers; this was true of Trimdon Motor Services, although it soon became a barracuda amid the minnows. Joe Grundy's business soon found itself allied with that of Paul & Seymour as both were pioneers of the Durham to West Hartlepool via Trimdon Grange service. By 1926 the two operators were coordinating their timetables and in 1928 jointly opened a second service, from Trimdon to Houghton-le-Spring. A complete merger seemed logical and Trimdon Motor Services Limited was registered in November 1929. In 1934 expansion came with the purchase of the County Bus Service with a route from Ferryhill to Durham, but such acquisitiveness was a rarity in the prewar years. The company's focus tended to be on growth by increasing frequencies, as in 1948 when the main service from Durham to West Hartlepool was doubled to run half-hourly. This was to change in 1953 when Messrs Grundy, Paul and Seymour sold the company to a consortium of local businessmen chaired by Tees-side motor-dealer J R Griffiths. Among the other new shareholders were the Brunskill family, haulage contractors from Bishop Auckland, who also controlled the bus company Direct Services which ran from Bishop Auckland to Middlesborough. In the following year the Trimdon Group acquired the business of Stewart, of Horden, and this gave them opportunities in Peterlee New Town which had been built astride Stewart's previously unimportant service. The influx of new capital led to thoughts of fleet renewal and these were given substance in 1954 when a deal was made with Sentinel for the provision of no fewer than ten vehicles, some of them new, others former demonstrators or unsold stock from previous years. The total included an STC6/44, four STC4/40s, three Beadle-bodied SLC4 coaches and two SLC6/30s with striking Coronation Land Cruiser bodywork by Associated Coach Builders, a local company. Anecdotal evidence suggests that a very hard bargain was struck by

Above: Whieldon of Rugeley, trading as Green Bus, operated a total of six Sentinels, but all had gone by 1957 and pictures of them in Whieldon livery are comparatively rare.. This is STC6/44 **YRF 732** at an unknown location but bound for its home base. The colours are dark green and medium grey. As far as is known only the Burlingham bodied SLC6/30 - pictured earlier - carried the later (and much more attractive) two-tone green and cream livery.

Below: Wigmore, of Dinnington, operated an important service into Sheffield city centre from their home village, and STC4/40 **JWW 316** is seen here operating a return leg. The main colour of the livery is medium blue, of a shade identical to that used on STC4/40 demonstrator GUJ 608. We suspect that the paint employed on GUJ 608 was originally ordered by Sentinel in the hope of more deliveries to Wigmore. It never happened and JWW 316 remained a one-off.

Trimdon's (car dealer) chairman but from Sentinel's viewpoint it had the dual advantages of clearing out the yard whilst giving the impression of a breakthrough sale to a major customer. By 1954 the fireworks of the original breakthrough (the Ribble order) had long since faded and the sales team were in need of a spectacular success, whatever the price. Trimdon must have been pleased, as they went on to buy further second-hand Sentinels. STC6/44s came from Owen, of Upper Boddington, and Riviera, of Mylor Bridge, while an additional STC4/40 arrived from Harries, of Prendergast. The net result of this was that Trimdon found itself with the second largest fleet of Sentinel PSVs in the country, out-distanced only by Ribble.

A major change in Trimdon's direction came in 1959 when the Griffiths/Brunskill consortium sold the company to another Teesside businessman, Mr Robert Lewis, who ordered a fleet of Thames Traders with bus bodywork by Duple (Midland). Although brand-new these were clearly inferior to the Sentinels in every regard except for fuel consumption, but this factor was allowed to become paramount and the better vehicles were driven out by the bad. It is hard to believe that Trimdon's passengers preferred the austere and noisy new buses or that drivers welcomed the constant swivelling motion necessary to collect fares from them as they boarded. The Sentinel fleet was scattered far and wide to the benefit of passengers elsewhere.

Vehicles: OUP 578 (STC6/44/100 - originally registered JNT 763) f/n 4, OUP 579 (STC4/40/73) f/n 14, OUP 580 (STC4/40/84) f/n 10, OUP 581 (STC4/40/17 - originally registered JUX 270) f/n 24, OUP 582 (STC4/40/83) f/n 26 and later f/n 22, PPT 212 (SLC4/35/66) f/n 5, PPT 213 (SLC4/27/3) f/n 9, PPT 214 (SLC4/27/4) f/n 7, PPT 690 (63011) f/n 3, PPT 850 (63010) f/n 39, ODE 40 (STC4/40/71) f/n 40, NNN 998 (STC6/44/94) f/n 11, YRF 733 (STC6/44/97) f/n 26 - fleet number previously used by OUP 582 which was renumbered.

WARNERS MOTORS LTD, Tewkesbury, Gloucestershire
The green-liveried vehicles of this fleet, some of them ageing but all well-kept, were a common sight at seaside resorts such as Bournemouth and Weston-super-Mare for many years. Closer to home the operator had a thriving business in contract work for schools and industry and also operated a pair of market-day services, from Tewkesbury to Chaceley and Strensham. These ran on Wednesdays and Saturdays, and in the late 1950s were the preserve of two second-hand Sentinel buses. The first of these, an STC4/40, was a former demonstrator which had passed to Maryland Luxury Coaches, London, before finding its way to Gloucestershire in 1955. In the following year it was joined by an SLC6/30 with Whitson bus bodywork which had served as a demonstrator for almost two years before purchase by Warners. The company was already familiar with the Sentinel marque as the manufacturer's coaches had featured in the fleet since 1951 when a new Beadle-bodied SLC4/35 had been delivered. This was followed in 1952 by an SLC6/41 with Plaxton Venturer superstructure. All four had been sold by 1960, but in early 1963 Warners bought a further two SLC6/30 coaches from the Bristol Co-operative Society. One of these had Plaxton bodywork, the other carried Whitson's elegant Grand Prix styling. Both had gone by the end of the year.

Vehicles: GUJ 608 (STC4/40/30), KDG 853 (SLC4/35/26), LDF 296 (SLC6/41/101), SDF 17 (63017), SHT 468 (6303), TAE 618 (63018).

WESTERN NATIONAL OMNIBUS COMPANY LTD, Exeter, Devonshire
Western National was formed in 1929 through the amalgamation of the local bus interests of the Great Western Railway and the National Omnibus and Transport Company. It later passed to Tilling and in 1948 entered the state-owned sector. From that point onwards most deliveries would be of Bristols with ECW bodywork, but in the early days of state control more leeway was allowed because of a shortage of manufacturing capacity. Thus, in the late 1940s, WNOC took delivery of a large number of Bedford OB coaches and also placed an order with J C Beadle for twelve buses of semi-integral construction employing Bedford engines and running units. This led to Western National agreeing to operate the second

Above: **NDE 799** was originally delivered to Edwards Brothers Motors, of Crymmych in Pembrokeshire, but was operating in the Bodmin area of Cornwall by the time of this photograph. The vehicle is in the yard of its new owner, Willis Central Garage, which ran infrequent local timings under the name Willis Services. After a short sojourn in Bodmin the vehicle was scrapped when barely ten years old.

Below: Yorkshire Traction fitted a destination-screen box to former Camplejohn STC6/44 **LWT 880**, seen in Barnsley in full YTC livery.

Sentinel-Beadle prototype, which arrived in Devonshire in early 1949. The vehicle operated on long-term hire from Sentinel (although registered in Devonshire as HOD 57 in the middle of a WNOC batch) and was eventually acquired in May 1952 after receiving an upgrade to direct injection. The Sentinel spent most of its time with WNOC in solitude, not only because of its unusual manufacturer but also through its allocation to the small depot at Sidmouth where WNOC had few services. Devon General territory lay to the west of the town and Southern National's area to the east. The Sentinel ran northwards across sparsely populated country to Taunton on the daily 278/279 services. It was withdrawn at the end of the 1958 summer season, and after passing through the hands of dealers in Yorkshire and Cheshire ended up with Sheriff in Lincolnshire.
Vehicle: HOD 57 (SB4/40/2).

C J & M A WHIELDON, Rugeley,
Staffordshire
C J Whieldon entered the bus industry as a driver for Stevensons, of Spath, but in 1927 he bought a 20-seat Reo and began his own operation, developing services from Uttoxeter to Lichfield and Rugeley. In 1930 the trading name Green Bus was adopted and the network grew to include a Uttoxeter to Stafford route and various local services to villages in the Uttoxeter, Cannock, Lichfield, and Rugeley areas. The Whieldon business had two brief but intense flirtations with Fodens, in 1933-5 and 1947-51, and then turned its gaze towards Shrewsbury for its first fleet of mid-engined vehicles and in the Spring of 1953 five Sentinels arrived at Rugeley. Two were former demonstrators, an STC4/40 and an STC6/44; the other three were brand-new STC6/44s. In late 1954 they were joined by a Burlingham-bodied SLC6/30 which had been one of six Sentinels on display at that year's Commercial Motor Show. All six vehicles were withdrawn in 1957 and dispersed to new operators in Kent, Cornwall and Yorkshire, replaced at Rugeley by an influx of second-hand double-deckers. Green Bus went on to run a fleet of Seddon Pennines (their engineers were never fazed by the unusual) and were eventually taken over by Midland Red in 1973.
Vehicles: GNT 190 (STC4/40/4) f/n 46, HUJ 619 (STC6/44/81) f/n 42, YRF 732 (STC6/44/93) f/n 43, YRF 733 (STC6/44/97) f/n 44, YRF 734 (STC6/44/99) f/n 45, 775 ERF (63012) f/n 47.

WHIPPET COACHES LTD, Hilton,
Huntingdonshire
In 1919 Mr H Lee, of Graveley, bought a Model T Ford ambulance and had it converted into a bus. From this modest beginning a major independent operator developed with daily services from St. Ives and Fenstanton to Cambridge along with several frequent village circulars in the Huntingdon area. Alongside these local routes an express service to London was operated, and the growth of RAF facilities in the area (particularly Wyton airfield) resulted in a doubling of passenger numbers in the 1940s and a concomitant increase in fleet size. A limited company was formed in 1953 and took the name the operator had long used for marketing purposes. Five years later an STC4/40 previously used by Delaine joined the already diverse fleet and was used mainly on the village circulars, although there is at least one report of it serving as a London express duplicate shortly after acquisition. After two years the vehicle was withdrawn and moved westwards to Mid-Wales Motorways where it later met a fiery end. Whippet continue to be one of the leading local bus operators in the region and have latterly developed a taste for MCW-Scania Metropolitan double-deckers.
Vehicle: GNT 961 (STC4/40/14).

A & C WIGMORE LTD, Dinnington, West
Yorkshire
Wigmore started a service from Dinnington to Sheffield via Thurcroft, Whiston, and Tinsley in the early 1930s with Leyland Lions and Tigers. The operator remained loyal to Leyland until 1961 with the exception of a few wartime Bedford OWB utility vehicles and a single Sentinel STC4/40, delivered new in April 1950. The vehicle was featured in Sentinel publicity of the time, and an SLC4/35 coach appeared in Wigmore livery at the 1950 Commercial Motor Show but this was never delivered, suggesting some dissatisfaction with the bus variant. Whatever the truth, the STC4/40 ran until the end of 1953, finding a new home the following year with Enterprise, in Somerset. From 1963

*Another modification involving a roof-box that radically altered the appearance of the front dome - not, perhaps, for the better. This is Burlingham-bodied SLC6/30 **775 ERF**, once a Commercial Motor Show exhibit. Its previous liveries, with Whieldon and then Camplejohn Brothers, had been among the most attractive around in the late 1950s and Yorkshire Traction's red and cream livery was rather bland in comparison.*

onwards Wigmore switched their allegiance to Bedfords and became well known for their frequent replacement of the fleet with new vehicles. The Dinnington service passed to Northern Bus after deregulation and formed the basis for that operator's mushrooming route network.
Vehicle: JWW 316 (STC4/40/15).

T W & T E WILLIAMS, Laugharne, Carmarthenshire
Tudor Williams started carrying passengers from his home village (later made famous by the poet Dylan Thomas) to the county town in 1908, using a horse-drawn wagonette. The operation switched to petrol power during the First World War when two Model T Fords were acquired, and in the same period the service was extended to run from Pendine. A second service from Carmarthen to Meidrim was developed during the 1920s, and the business began to use the trading name of Pioneer. Although this was painted on the side of the buses most locals well into the 1960s referred to their village operator as Tudor Williams and the company's letterhead pronounced it to be Tudor Williams Brothers & Sons. Whatever its true title, the business appears to have operated a Sentinel STC6/44 although authoritative reports of it in actual service have proven elusive. The vehicle in question had previously been operated by Riviera in the Falmouth area but had been new to Whieldon in Rugeley. If it did in fact operate with Tudor Williams (it received the company's fleetnames) it appears to have gone by the end of 1966 without having made much of an impression.
Vehicle: YRF 734 (STC6/44/99).

WILLIS CENTRAL GARAGE LTD, Bodmin, Cornwall
Trading as Willis Services, this local motor dealer operated a circular service from Bodmin town centre to the villages of Blisland, Cardinham and Mount, with most journeys timed to attract schoolchildren rather than

commuters. The Willis routes were informally coordinated with those of Webber, who ran over much of the same routes, albeit with timings more suited to shopping expeditions. In March 1958 the company acquired a second-hand Sentinel previously owned by Edwards Brothers Motors, of Crymmych. This was used on the stage carriage service until its withdrawal just over two years later - its ultimate fate remains unrecorded. In 1976 the Willis business was taken over by its old associates at Webber Brothers, of Blisland, and the elimination of unnecesary overheads left Webber in a stronger position to expand when deregulation loomed. By then the Willis name meant nothing more than a car dealership.
Vehicle: NDE 799 (STC4/40/24).

R D WOOLLEY & V K ENGLISH, Haccombe, Devonshire

In 1963 Potter, of Haytor (qv), discontinued their famous Tor Bus service from Newton Abbot to Widecombe and Messrs Woolley and English - partners in a local private-hire operation - stepped in to preserve this essential rural amenity. Trading as the Dartmoor Bus Company, they used their existing vehicle (a Harrington-bodied Foden) and a newly acquired SLC4/35 with a pedigree that began with the Bristol Co-op, but neither of these machines proved very reliable when used on daily services amid the wilds of Dartmoor. Within a few months the brave venture had come to an end and the Widecombe route had become Devon General's service 23.
Vehicle: NHY 465 (SLC4/35/53).

YORKSHIRE TRACTION COMPANY LTD, Barnsley, West Yorkshire

BET subsidiary Yorkshire Traction acquired its three Sentinels (along with two Atkinsons and a Dennis Lancet) through the purchase of Camplejohn Brothers, of Darfield (qv), in January 1961. All these unorthodox vehicles were pressed into service by their new owners, making YTC the third BET company to operate Sentinels. The two STC6/44s were kept until February 1963, the end of their natural lifespan by BET parameters, and were then resold to A.A. Motor Services in Ayrshire (qv). The SLC6/30 then became unique and as a result was withdrawn, after only ten years on the road, in December 1964. It ran for five more years with two independent operators before its demise in 1969.
Vehicles: HAW 577 (STC6/44/82) f/n 129C, LWT 880 (STC6/44/89) f/n 130C, 775 ERF (63012) f/n 132C.

NON-PSV USERS

In later life many Sentinels found employment away from the hurly-burly of the Public Service Vehicle arena, experiencing second careers in easier conditions. A vehicle with an estimated service life of a year or less, and that if only used sparingly, was of little interest to bus and coach operators, but could represent an irresistible bargain to a contractor. Such vehicles, used as private staff transport, might be on the road for twelve hours a week or less, and did not incur the expensive maintenance regimen inflicted upon vehicles licensed for hire. Needless to say, fleet turnover was high, and most of the once-proud PSVs which found their way to contractors would leave them bound for the scrapyard.

Staff buses

Of the 26 Sentinels known to have passed into non-PSV usage, ten, the largest group by far, were used as staff transport. Former Ribble STC6/44s were prominent, with examples in use with companies in Blackpool, Formby, and Lowton (all in Lancashire), Mansfield Woodhouse (Nottinghamshire) and Gillingham (in Kent), where Parham took an extra one to serve as a source of spares. Ribble's four-cylinder buses were less popular, although CRN 216 did serve with Norwest Construction in the Sheffield area as a site hut.

More mobile were STC4/40s GRP 105, the former K.W. Services machine, which turned up with Whittingham, a Wolverhampton contractor, and OUP 581, one of Trimdon's vehicles, which ended its active life with a company in Halifax. One of Trimdon's Beadle-bodied coaches, PPT 212, was exported to Ireland for private use there, but this may have been employed by a scout group or similar rather than as a company staff bus.

Apart from CRN 216 mentioned above, two other Sentinels gave service as immobile site-

Above: Liverpool-based Norwest Construction bought this former Ribble STC4/40, **CRN 216**, from dealer Frank Cowley. The vehicle was towed to a location near Sheffield where it was used as a site hut for a Norwest work crew. Note the water tank connected to the rear of the vehicle.

Below: This vehicle had been intended as a left-hand drive demonstrator for Sentinel's Dutch distributor but it was completed and registered JUX 270 for use as a UK demonstrator. However, the STC4/40 programme was terminated shortly after this vehicle's completion and it went on hire to Trimdon Motor Services *(see page 148)* who eventually bought it and reregistered it **OUP 581**. After sale by Trimdon it spent three months in Bristol with Hallen Coaches and then returned to the North as a staff bus with Hoyle, of Halifax. They painted it in the livery shown and kept it in service for almost three years.

huts. NNN 998, an STC6/44 originally ordered by Leon of Finningley but actually delivered to Owen in Northamptonshire, had passed through the hands of Trimdon Motor Services and Jordans, of Blaenavon, before arriving at the Pennington yard of dealer Frank Cowley, ostensibly as a spares source. However, it next appeared at the Liverpool premises of Norwest Construction, where it remained in use as a shed until finally scrapped.

The other Sentinel hut, LOD 974, managed to escape that fate. An STC4/40, built for Tor Bus in 1950, it saw use by two smaller Devonshire independents before vanishing at the end of the 1950s. More than twenty years later it turned up in a government surplus auction, having long been used as a mess-hut at Porton Down in Wiltshire. These premises are generally described as "germ-warfare laboratories" when mentioned in the press, but the Sentinel had (reassuringly?) been used by a unit known as the Civil Defence Establishment. Presumably defence against germ-warfare. It survives in preservation.

Mobile shops

The very first Sentinel diesel bus, SB4/40 EUJ 792, had an uneventful first decade, plodding the rural routes around Whitchurch, Shrewsbury, and Market Drayton in the rather insipid livery of Salopia Saloon Coaches. After retirement (replaced by a bus-bodied Bedford SB) it suffered the further indignity of being converted into a mobile shop. It operated as such in the Shrewsbury area and it seems a great shame that nobody locally thought to preserve it in its city of birth.

Third prototype CRN 211 suffered a similar fate after withdrawal by Ribble, passing from Frank Cowley to a gentleman who used it as a mobile shop in the Kenilworth area of Warwickshire. It seems strangely ironic that this landmark vehicle was destined for the scrapyard - Kenilworth is now the home of the country's leading Sentinel preservationist; sadly, the timing was not quite right.

Ribble's CRN 215 also found work in the retail trade with an owner in Widnes, while similar vehicle NDE 620 (new to Roberts, of Newport) was reported performing the same duties in Staffordshire and another (ODE 40, ex Harries and Trimdon) operated as a shop in Stockton-on-Tees. Four-cylinder variety was provided by PPT 214, a former Trimdon SLC4/27 which did business with Valley Supply of Bacup, Lancashire, and by HEA 433, a Plaxton Venturer-bodied SLC4/35 which became a mobile shop in Lincolnshire. Lastly, YRF 733, an STC6/44 new to Whieldon's Green Bus, Rugeley, but later with Riviera, Trimdon and Milson of Coningsby, passed first to Powell, of Ellesmere Port (who used it on works services to the Stanlow oil refinery) and then to an unidentified owner for use as a mobile shop on the nearby Wirral peninsula.

Conversions on the road

Perhaps the most unusual second career enjoyed by a Sentinel was that of the former Simmons (Reliance) STC6/44 GCT 181, which was converted into a mobile church and reported as far afield as Leicester and Bristol. Another oddity to be found at the time was the famous STC6/44 cafe, DRN 344, ex Ribble via Sproat, of Bedford, which plied its trade at Broadmarsh bus station in Nottingham for a while, much to the delight of visiting enthusiasts.

A more radical conversion was carried out on HUJ 619, a former demonstrator, which ran with Green Bus in Staffordshire and Riviera/Lewis in Cornwall. In February 1966 it was sighted at Exmouth in Devonshire cut down to a flat-bed apart from the cab and entrance area which retained the front dome. The object of this vandalism was to make the vehicle suitable for carrying stock-cars.

Two SLC6/30s also ended up as stock-car transporters, although retaining most of their original bodywork. Whitson bus-bodied SDF 17 had operated with Warners, of Tewkesbury, and Talbott, of Moreton-in-the-Marsh, before conversion by an owner in the West Midlands. A more up-market conversion was carried out on Duple Elizabethan example PXE 761, once the pride of the Lewis, of Greenwich, fleet. Although modified at the rear end to accommodate a stock-car, the forward half of the vehicle retained some of its luxury seating and was equipped with other creature comforts for a hard day at the stock-car races. The vehicle was later rescued for preservation by

Above: Ribble STC6/44 **DRN 344** passed to Sproat (Cedar Coaches), of Bedford, who painted it in a medium-red and cream livery. In its later and more famous guise as a mobile café in the Nottingham area it was often to be found at Broad Marsh bus station. Note the canopy at the rear of the vehicle which sheltered those waiting at the takeaway counter. We have been unable to trace the vehicle's operator despite its brief celebrity among enthusiasts. *(See also page 146.)*

Below: K.W. Services STC4/40, **GRP 105**, was sold to Staffordshire operator Gee and Harrison in 1958, did three years with them (largely on railway-related work) and then passed to Whittingham, the Wolverhampton-based contractor, for use as a staff bus. They used it for a further two years.

Above: This is the former Simmons vehicle **GCT 181** (pictured earlier in full Reliance livery). After retirement from Grantham local services it was sold to Roy's, of Nottingham, and from there to the dealer W S Yeates. An enterprising salesman sold it to the Reverend Waddington who operated the vehicle in both the Leicester and Bristol areas (and possibly elsewhere) as part of a Christian recruitment drive.

Below: Until this photograph arrived (courtesy of Colin Caddy) our records on STC6/44 **HUJ 619** ended with its retirement by Riviera. As this shot proves it had a later career as a stock-car transporter, drastically cut down to lorry format. The picture was taken at Exmouth, Devon, in February 1966; after that date there are no reports of this rather strange conversion.

Above: STC6/44 **NNN 998** had served with operators in Northamptonshire, County Durham and Monmouthshire before arriving engineless at the Pennington yard of Frank Cowley and being sold as seen to Norwest Construction for use as a storage shed. The vehicle is seen here at Norwest's Liverpool depot with STC4/40 **CRN 216**; a Bristol LWL/ECW coach; and a BMC J2 minibus.

Below: **GUX 614** was the very first STC6/44 demonstrator. It appeared at the 1950 Commercial Motor Show in ersatz Ribble livery and with the imaginary fleet number 266. It was later sold to Llynfi, of Maesteg, who operated it on their local service in South Wales for just over six years before trading it in to Don Everall. Here we see it with its next owner, Wootton, of Wombwell in the West Riding of Yorkshire, in use as a staff bus.

Spiers, the well-known Henley-upon-Thames bus and coach operator.

Another SLC6/30, the former Earls Court exhibit 657 CMT, had a long front-line career with Best and Son, of Wembley, and then with Willesden Coaches (also controlled by members of the Best family), before passing to a Mr Smith in Leighton Buzzard in 1965. Conflicting reports suggest that it was either converted to a motor-caravan, or underwent a similar conversion to that of PXE 761 with a stock-car entrance at the rear end. Photographic evidence is unavailable to determine the truth, but it was certainly licensed as a private vehicle for at least two years after leaving Willesden. It seems a great shame that it failed to survive into preservation, especially as no example of the magnificent Whitson Grand Prix body appears to have been preserved.

DERELICTS AND DEALERS

By the middle of the 1960s Sentinels in regular usage were becoming a rare sight, even by the standards of a type that was never that common outside of certain towns such as Carlisle, Durham and Falmouth. The Brown fleet continued in service into the early 1970s, but Telford New Town was a long way from the beaten track for most bus enthusiasts despite the lure of the exotic rota operators.

Fortunately, old Sentinels had a tendency to linger for a while. The two STC4/40s acquired by Morgan (Blue Line) with the business of Richardson (Majestic Motors) provide the most outstanding example of this. Unloved by their new owners, who preferred the combination of Guy chassis and Gardner engines, their indirect injection engines (this pair went unmodified) made them more trouble than they were worth and at their first major mechanical failures they were delicensed and placed into open storage at the Stainforth premises of Reliance (Blue Line's sister company in the Wilson group). This was in 1955/8. They were still there, slowly decaying, in 1962 and the most tenacious of the two hulks survived until a yard-tidying exercise finally eliminated it in 1971.

Sentinels going cheap

Another likely place to see a Sentinel in the 1960s was in the corner of a dealer's yard, with almost every major bus and coach dealer in the British Isles having handled at least one. They had usually been taken in part-exchange and then proved difficult to resell, especially after TVW withdrew from the supply of spares in the early 1960s.

Three dealerships actively specialised in Sentinels during the 1960s. Stanley Hughes and Company of Bradford (with yards at Gomersal and Mirfield) bought most of the Trimdon Motor Services fleet, consisting of three STC6/44s (two had been acquired second-hand by Trimdon), four STC4/40s, three four-cylinder coaches and the two SLC6/30s with A.C.B. coachwork. These were all successfully resold, passing to new operators in Lanarkshire, Northumberland, Yorkshire, Lancashire, Lincolnshire, and Staffordshire. Hughes had a working relationship with the Monmouthshire dealer Cowdell, of Newport, who sold one of the Trimdon STC6/44s to Jordans, of Blaenavon, but were less lucky with SLC4/27 PPT 214, which ended up returning to Bradford before resale as a staff bus.

Hughes were also responsible for the disposal of the three former Schofield SLC6/30s taken into stock by Hanson, and of the similar UUB 931 which had been the only Sentinel in the fleet of Wallace Arnold Tours (as opposed to the dealership). These were all equipped with Burlingham Seagull bodywork which helped them to find new owners without much difficulty.

Apart from the Trimdon machines and the aforementioned Seagulls only one other Sentinel appears to have been handled by Hughes: LNY 307, one of the two SLC4/35s with Gurney Nutting bodywork. This arrived from Dawlish Coaches in Devon and was resold to Fenwick in Lincolnshire, giving Hughes a grand total of 17 Sentinels.

Cowley for Sentinel

Frank Cowley's head office was in Blackfriars Road, Salford, and had a parking space for one vehicle, although others were sometimes to be found in nearby side streets. The vast bulk of

Above: **GNT 587** started its life as an STC4/40 demonstrator and was then sold to Richardson (Majestic Motors), of Thorne, in 1952. The following year it passed (along with Richardson's stage services) to Samuel Morgan, of Armthorpe, more popularly known as Blue Line. Morgan was profoundly unimpressed with the brace of indirect-injection Sentinels (among the few that were never updated) and retired them as quickly as possible. The vehicles were then left in the open but proved sturdy enough to last for more than a decade, to the delight of both local wildlife and visiting bus enthusiasts. The location is the Stainforth yard of Blue Line's sister company, Premier.

Below: And this is the other former Richardson STC4/40, also at Stainforth after early retirement. **GUJ 457** had been allocated for delivery to Cooper, of Oakengates, but remained with the manufacturer as a demonstrator, still in Cooper livery. The remainder of its history was identical to that of GNT 587.

the dealership's stock was to be found in its other yards, at Fallowfield in south Manchester, at Pennington (in the parish of Lowton, near Leigh in Lancashire) and at Dunchurch in Warwickshire.

In 1963 Cowley became the major player in the used Sentinel business through the acquisition of all 19 surviving Ribble examples (CRN 214 had been scrapped locally after its engine fire at Bowness-on-Solway). The buses, one SB4/40 prototype, four STC4/40s and fourteen STC6/44s, had all arrived at Pennington by the end of 1963 with several continuing on to the Dunchurch yard to attract customers in the Midlands.

The four-cylinder vehicles proved almost impossible to unload, but customers were found for most of the STC6/44s, six going to contractors and others being sold for further PSV service with operators in Yorkshire, Bedfordshire, Dorset, Caernarvonshire and Glamorgan.

Available records show four other Sentinels passing through Cowley's hands. The very first was STC4/40, NDE 555, which arrived from South Wales (Morrison, of Tenby) and was immediately sold in North Wales (Bellis, of Buckley). Despite this rapid turnaround, two and a half years elapsed before Cowley's next Sentinel arrived, and this was a beast of a very different nature. MYV 637 was an SLC6/42 with Bellhouse-Hartwell Landmaster bodywork incorporating 32 luxurious seats, a toilet compartment, and a galley for basic food preparation. One can only presume that Frank Cowley put his best salesman to work on this one, although at least its 33-foot length was no longer a problem from 1961 onwards. The vehicle was eventually sold to Mandator Coaches who planned to use it on overland tours to India, although there seems to be some doubt that these were ever operated. Shortly afterwards the other Blue Cars B-H bodied Sentinel, SLC6/41 NLR 850, came onto the dealership's books and was quickly resold to Moore, of Great Witley.

Cowley's fourth Sentinel, the last to arrive before the deluge of Ribble machines, was the engineless NNN 998, an STC6/44, which arrived at Pennington on a lowloader from Jordans, of Blaenavon in Monmouthshire, and was resold to Norwest Construction of Liverpool to serve as a shed. This humble machine brought Cowley's grand total up to twenty-three over the nine-year period in which they dealt in the marque.

Jack of all trades

The Don Everall group have been involved in most aspects of the passenger transport industry over the years, ranging from the well-known operation of coaches and double-deckers to the ownership of a small scheduled airline in the 1950s. Another aspect of their activities has been a PSV dealership based at a yard in Wolverhampton, justifiably famous among bus enthusiasts for the rare types which regularly passed through. It seemed that Everalls would buy anything, but equally could also sell anything. Sentinels became something of a speciality.

Whereas Hughes and Cowley had acquired most of their Sentinels as job lots, Everalls acquired theirs in ones and twos, usually in part exchange. The largest single transaction involved the purchase of two STC4/40s from Gee and Harrison, of Whittington, who had used them on contract works services in the Lichfield area of Staffordshire. One went to a local contractor, the other was sold to Phillips, of Glyn Ceiriog, who returned it after a few months - the terrain of their route was fundamentally unsuitable for an ageing four-cylinder bus of any make. Everall sold it again, this time to Longstaff in the West Riding who decided to keep it.

All three of the Llynfi Motors six-cylinder Sentinel buses were acquired over 18 months in three different transactions. One of these was STC6/44 GUX 614, the 1950 Earls Court vehicle, still carrying the fictitious Ribble fleet number 266 on its forward bulkhead. It passed to a contractor in Yorkshire. Another was STC6/44 GTH 576, originally delivered to Davies Brothers, of Pencader. Everalls found it a customer even further west, selling it to the Princess Bus Service, of Clonmel in the Republic of Ireland. The third member of the Llynfi trio, former SLC6/30 demonstrator KUX 412, carried unique A.C.B. bus bodywork and had been modified from dual-door to single-door at some stage in its career. These were far from positive selling points, but the

Above: Ribble's **DRN 352** passed to the Frank Cowley dealership along with its thirteen STC6/44 siblings. It was used briefly by a contractor, Croston, of Lowton, but remained based at Cowley's Pennington yard and was soon delicensed. It remained unsold and was broken up for spares.

Below: As mentioned in an earlier caption, STC4/40 **NDE 620** saw service with a Welsh operator (Roberts), an English one (Martin), and a Scottish one (Simpson, of Cardenden in Fife). It then passed into the hands of the dealer Don Everall and is seen here through the fence at their main Wolverhampton yard. The destination blind is a mystery as Scarborough would not have appeared on the blinds used by any of its known operators and it subsequently became a mobile shop.

Above: An SLC6/41 with Bellhouse-Hartwell Landmaster bodywork, **NLR 850**, which started its career with Blue Cars but by the time of this photograph had been withdrawn by its final owner, Moore, of Great Witley (Glider Coaches). The location is Moore's depot and the vehicle was scrapped shortly afterwards.

Below: Originally a member of the Trimdon fleet, **PPT 212** ended up with an unidentified non-PSV user in the Republic of Ireland and passed from them to this scrapyard near Edgeworthstown, County Cork. It survived there in relatively intact condition until 2002 when it was scrapped a matter of weeks before a rescue mission by U.K. preservationists.

vehicle found a niche with Simpson of Cardenden in Fife.

A year or so later Simpson sold an earlier Sentinel purchase, STC4/40 NDE 620, to Everall and this was eventually converted into a mobile shop. This was also the eventual fate of STC6/44 YRF 733, but it passed through Everall's hands in between Milson, of Coningsby, and Powell, of Ellesmere Port, who (as previously mentioned) bought it for contract works services on the Mersey estuary's Costa del Chemicals.

There were also SLC4/35s to be seen in the Wolverhampton yard. One of the Bristol Co-op machines (NHY 637) arrived in poor condition after an accident while in service with Smith, of Corby Glen, and was subsequently scrapped. Another BCS vehicle, PAE 596, had better luck, arriving from Bugler Coaches, Bristol, and leaving in the hands of John, of Tonypandy, for further service. Gurney Nutting-bodied example LNY 307 was a later arrival from Smith, of Corby Glen, and was scrapped after failing to sell - it had stood in the open for some time at Corby Glen without turning a wheel.

The most interesting Everall purchase was undoubtedly LDF 296, an SLC6/41 with Plaxton Venturer coachwork originally built for Warners of Tewkesbury. They sold it to Talbott (Barry's Coaches), of Moreton-in-the-Marsh, but it was evidently not quite what they had in mind as it had passed to Everall within weeks. The dealership duly resold it to Browns (Falcon Coaches), of Baillieston in Scotland, who seemed reasonably satisfied with it and kept it for sixteen months before trading it back in to Everall for something newer. Having sold it to a Scottish operator, Everall went for the set by selling it next to the Welsh operator Prance, of Cardiff. They were less than impressed and returned it to the dealer within the warranty period. Everall then sold it to Dudley, of Inkberrow in Worcestershire, but they too returned it within weeks. It then went to Cray Coaches, of St. Pauls Cray in Kent, who kept it for four months before sending it back to Wolverhampton. At that point even Don Everall gave up on it and it was left in a dark corner for a year or so before being scrapped.

SENTINELS IN PRESERVATION

The oldest Sentinel bus in preservation is the 1938 Sentinel-HSG prototype based upon a Gilford 176 chassis and registered AUX 296. Fitted with a Cowieson (of Glasgow) body, it appeared at the 1938 Scottish Show and was operated on loan by both Merthyr Tydfil Corporation and South Wales Transport before the experiment was brought to an end by the start of the Second World War. By 1942 it had been converted to petrol power and sold to local Shropshire independent Cooper, of Oakengates.

Cooper kept it in service until at least 1959 (some sources say 1960) before retiring it and then made further use of it as a storage unit at the garage. It survived in increasingly derelict condition until 1976 when it was rescued by a Mr Heslop, of Hexham in Northumberland. It later passed to Alan Purvis, of Seaburn, who sadly fell ill and died before he could restore the vehicle, and it is now owned by Mr R Wallace, of Edinburgh. It is currently located at the Scottish Vintage Bus Museum at Lathalmond, Fife.

A Sentinel in Birmingham

The only other Sentinel PSV currently located within a museum is STC4/40 demonstrator GUJ 608 which is kept at Aston Manor Transport Museum in Birmingham by its owner, Mr Richard Gray. This vehicle, new in November 1950, was later sold to M & H Leader (trading as Maryland Luxury Coaches), a local private hire operator in east London, and was then resold to Warners of Tewkesbury, Gloucestershire, in December 1955. After three years in that Sentinel-friendly fleet, it passed to Browns, of Donnington Wood, for use on the Telford rotas, a task it performed for another twelve years before withdrawal in 1971. After a short period in open storage it was purchased by Mr Gray who chose to restore it in the livery of Maryland. The vehicle is usually to be found on public display at the Aston Manor facility.

The Herefordshire collection

Richard Gray was not the only preservationist to head for Donnington. Mr D L Wheatley, of

Kenilworth in Warwickshire, also made the pilgrimage, buying SLC4/35 HAW 373 in December 1971 and similar vehicles HAW 302 and HNT 101 two years later. All had been modified to front entrance layout by Browns, and Mr Wheatley was given the sliding door and other body parts from HAW 374 which had retained its central entrance but was otherwise in poor condition. These were needed so that HAW 373 could be restored to as new condition, a process that continues as time allows. HAW 302 was originally intended as a spares source but remains basically intact (although without passenger seats) while further spare parts were obtained from sister vehicle HNT 101 which remained at Donnington Wood until dismantled.

Meanwhile, Mr Wheatley and fellow preservationist Martin Perry (the Bromyard-based bus and coach entrepreneur) had acted decisively to save another four-cylinder Sentinel coach, NWO 122. This was of the later SLC4/27 variant and spent its entire working life with the Monmouthshire independent Chapple, of Raglan. As was the practice with that operator, it spent its early years on private hire and excursion work before being relegated to the restricted works services operated for coalminers in the area. By 1973 the vehicle was in a scrapyard in Gloucestershire whence it was rescued by Messrs Wheatley and Perry. It remains in unrestored condition.

Already in possession of three Sentinels, Mr Wheatley added a fourth in January 1982 when he acquired former Browns SLC4/35 HNT 49. This had been withdrawn by the operator in 1971 and had passed through the hands of at least two private owners, one a Reading-based syndicate of trolleybus enthusiasts who had stored it at Sandtoft for a while. In Mr Wheatley's ownership it moved to the BaMMOT Museum at Wythall to the south of Birmingham, where it had a belated reunion with its sibling, HAW 373, although both machines had left Wythall by the end of the decade.

Almost twenty years later, in October 2001, Mr Wheatley acquired a fifth Sentinel, this time an SLC6/30 coach with Burlingham Seagull bodywork. SUG 19 had briefly been a Wallace Arnold demonstrator before sale to Metcalfe, of Keighley. Eight owners later it found itself in very sorry condition amongst vegetation in a yard at Stondon in Essex. Worse yet, the yard was about to be cleared and the vehicle was in need of urgent rescue. Fortunately a Mr Plant, of Sale in Cheshire, stepped into the breach and then resold the Sentinel to Mr Wheatley, who transported it to Herefordshire. As may be imagined, the vehicle is in a bad way and a gargantuan effort will be needed if it is to be restored to its former glory.

All five of these machines are now kept at a private location in the county of Herefordshire and work continues on the restoration of HAW 373 and HNT 49 with the intention that the former vehicle be restored to its original configuration and the latter as the final one-man-operated version. Mr Wheatley is to be congratulated for his many years of dedication to these vehicles and we look forward to their debut on the rally circuit in years to come. We would also urge all and sundry to offer their assistance in helping to preserve and restore this invaluable collection of pioneering PSVs. Mr Wheatley can be contacted via the authors c/o the publisher's Glossop address.

A legend from Dartmoor

Sentinel enthusiasts had long mourned the loss of the famous Tor Bus STC4/40 LOD 974, surely one of the most attractive examples of the breed, which had disappeared from view in the late 1950s and had thus been presumed scrapped. This was not the case, as the vehicle had found its way from Heard, of Hartland (its last operator), to the military establishment at Porton Down in Wiltshire. In 1980 it re-emerged into the public arena at a military surplus auction and was fortunately noticed by preservationist Colin Shears who secured it for his West of England Transport Collection.

In 1981 the vehicle was sold on to a preservation group specifically created for its restoration. This process quickened when the group received a grant of ten thousand pounds from the Pools Promoters' Association charity, and this generous assistance along with the handiwork of local craftsmen has seen the vehicle restored to Tor Bus livery. By 1997 it was roadworthy and making appearances at village fetes in Devonshire, much to the delight of locals who remember both the the bus and its operator with great affection. As of last report a set of suitable seats had been found and a full internal restoration was planned. We imagine that the completed vehicle will be enormously popular at running days in the near future.

A Welsh Sentinel in Yorkshire

Although there are two superbly preserved STC4/40 buses, the larger STC6/44 has been less fortunate and only one is confirmed as being safe in preservation. The vehicle known to be secure is ODE 182, which was new to Edwards Brothers Motors, of Crymmych in Pembrokeshire, in March 1952. In 1957 the business was purchased by Messrs Rees and Phillips who restyled it as Midway Motors and the STC6/44's livery was amended accordingly. Withdrawn from service in May 1963, it was placed into open storage alongside the depot and by 1974 was in use as a storage shed. Ten years later a visitor to the site reported its condition as derelict, but in 1990 the hulk of the vehicle was rescued by preservationist Peter Bowers and transported to a new home in Berkshire.

Little work was done on the vehicle, and in 1998 Mr Bowers sold it to John Hinchliffe, the well-known Yorkshire enthusiast who is a leading light in the Huddersfield Passenger Transport Group. An epic journey from Berkshire ensued, which included the marvellous sight of an STC6/44 parked on the hard shoulder of the M25 Motorway, but the machine eventually arrived at its new home "underneath the arches" without further incident.

The original engine proved impossible to save (but a replacement has been created through the conversion of a 4-cylinder unit from a Sentinel generator lorry), while the bodywork has rotted in several key areas and will need extensive work. Nevertheless Mr Hinchliffe remains confident that the vehicle will take to the road again in years to come, reviving many memories of Yorkshire Sentinels operated by Camplejohn, Yorkshire Traction, Baddeley Brothers, Longstaff, Schofields and Hanson, all of which once operated within a fifteen-mile radius of the STC6/44's current location. At present the vehicle is sitting quietly alongside the HPTG's

Tor Bus's magnificent STC4/40 **LOD 974** *returned from the dead to become the pride of a preservation group in its native Devonshire. Here it is parked alongside some cars which would have seemed like science-fiction vehicles when the Sentinel was in its youth.*

131

forward entrance Daimler CVG6 awaiting its own place in the spotlight at future events.

A restored Elizabethan

Stock-car racing may not be the sport of kings, nor the preferred recreation of most bus enthusiasts, but several extremely rare vehicles have survived into preservation as a result of second careers as stock-car transporters. Among them is PXE 761, a Sentinel SLC6/30 with Duple Elizabethan bodywork modified at the rear end to allow the carriage of a car as well as its driver, mechanics, and several lucky supporters in the more conventional front end. A far cry from October 1954 when it appeared at the Commercial Motor Show in the livery of Lewis, of Greenwich.

In its original form the vehicle was particularly luxurious, having been built to the order of Sentinel distributor Wiggs (Grey Coaches) as a demonstrator. Wiggs were the subject of a takeover bid before the vehicle could be delivered and Duple sold the surplus machine to Lewis who already had a pair of similar Elizabethan-bodied Sentinels. Company records show that Lewis part-exchanged two Bedford OB/Duple Vistas for their new coach. Lewis kept the coach for more than a decade before selling it to Seth of London NW5 in 1966. A year later it apparently disappeared, re-emerging in non-PSV guise in 1971 when it was sold to the Simpson Engineering company, of Brixham in Devonshire, for use as a stock-car transporter. By 1981 it was performing this function with a Mr Jolly in Hampshire, sporting a rather fetching colour scheme of overall burgundy with light blue wheel-arch mouldings, and by 1990 was in Bristol with Mr J Bronson. In 1995 it was purchased by Spiers of Henley for preservation. Recent reports suggest that it may have changed hands again, still with its modified rear end but otherwise in good condition. More information on this machine's present location and ownership would be very welcome and should be sent to the authors at the address given in the introduction.

The one that got away

Nine diesel-powered Sentinel PSVs are known to survive (with the possibility of a tenth lurking somewhere in Ireland), but several others narrowly missed preservation. Probably the most annoying example of this is Beadle-bodied SLC4/35 PPT 212, which started life with Trimdon Motor Services in 1954 although originally ordered by Morgan of Corse Lawn who cancelled it before delivery.

After service with Trimdon the vehicle passed to a local Tees-side independent for a few weeks, but was returned and resold to Ford, of Ackworth, in August 1960. They were also unimpressed and sold it on to the Hughes dealership in Bradford four months later. In May 1961 it turned up in Glasgow operating for Blackmore before being exported to Ireland where it was first reported in 1966. Although retaining its full complement of coach seats, it was apparently operated on a private tax-disc so it might be guessed that its unknown owner was a church or sporting club. Whatever the truth it was next reported as withdrawn from use in February 1968, languishing within sight of the road at Edgeworthstown, County Cork.

Amazingly, it was still there in 2001, basically intact if somewhat weatherbeaten, and Trimdon Motor Services expert Phillip Kirk began negotiations with the scrap-dealer to repatriate the vehicle to England. Sadly these efforts came to nothing and the Sentinel was finally scrapped during 2002, bringing to an end any hope of preserving a vehicle from the thirteen-strong Trimdon fleet. One can only hope that the rumours of STC6/44 GTH 576's survival prove to be correct and that the vehicle (if it still exists) can be ushered into the public gaze before suffering a similar fate to PPT 212, the lesser known of the only two Irish Sentinels.

Above: Owned by David L Wheatley and seen at its Herefordshire base, **HNT 49** is one of a number of former Browns (of Donnington Wood) vehicles preserved. This is a 1951 Beadle-bodied coach which spent its entire life with the operator. It was latterly converted to front-entrance and fitted with bus seats, features which are currently retained. *(D L Wheatley)*

Below: **PXE 761** was the Duple-bodied exhibit at the 1954 Commercial Motor Show. After twelve years as a PSV it was converted to a stock car transporter and used thus until 1990. It was then acquired by a Mr Spiers, of Henley on Thames, whose company ran Sentinel coaches in the 1950s (but not this one). It was intended that it be reconverted to a coach when time,(and parts), permitted but there have been no recent progress reports.

Above: **ODE 182** is the only remaining 6-cylinder Sentinel bus. It is currently being rebuilt by John Hincliffe in Huddersfield. New in 1952, it served the area around Crymmych in South Wales until May 1963. On withdrawal it was parked beside the depot until retrieved by Peter Bowers and taken to Berkshire in 1990. Unable to commence its restoration, he sold it to John Hinchliffe in 1998. It is seen minus a wheel on the M25 when in transit from Berkshire to Huddersfield. The picture is a graphic illustration of the task facing the preservationist of a long derelict vehicle. *(John Hinchliffe)*

Below: Plaxton Venturer-bodied SLC6/41 **LDF 296**, once the star of a Sentinel trade advertisement in its original Warner, of Tewkesbury, livery, is seen here in the colours of Brown (Falcon Coaches), Baillieston, in the early 1960s.

Above: Lewis, of Greenwich, were the first owners of this Duple Elizabethan-bodied SLC6/30, **OXT 23**. It is seen here with its second owner, Roberts, of Llanberis in North Wales. It ended its life at a kennels in Kent.

Below: One of only two Sentinels fitted with the later style of Plaxton Venturer bodywork, this SLC6/30 was new to Bluebird Garages, of Hull, and received the registration **RAT 645**. After withdrawal by them it passed to P. & M. Coach Line in Ipswich and then served with Cook of Braintree and Cutting of Brockley before arriving at the premises of the Arlington dealership in Sudbury where this photograph was taken in May 1966.

Above: Burlingham Seagull-bodied SLC6/30 OWU 771 was one of the Schofield quartet but is seen here with a later operator, Gee Cross Motors, at their Stalybridge premises. The side mouldings, as with the other Schofield machines, are of the Seagull Mark Two variety and presumably represent 'leftovers' as this design had been deleted before the Sentinels were built.

Below: Bellis, of Buckley in North Wales, bought this former Morrison, of Tenby, STC4/40 for schools work but nevertheless painted it in full livery. NDE 555 stayed with them for less than a year before resale to Henry Hulley of Baslow.

Registration Number Index

This listing includes all known Sentinel PSV chassis, including those converted from goods vehicles in prewar days, the one-off Sentinel-HSG, and postwar PSV variants which received an assortment of non-PSV bodywork. United Kingdom examples are listed first, in sequential alpha-numeric order (reversed registrations are treated as if presented with the letters first), and are followed by export vehicles listed by country of registration. Sentinel construction numbers from the prewar steam-waggon sequence are indicated by an asterisk *.

United Kingdom

Reg	Chassis
AUX 296	HSG.H1502
AW 3918	???? *
AYJ 822	STC4/40/12
BEJ 190	SLC4/35/21
BEP 864	STC4/40/16
CCB 584	SLC4/35/19
CCB 673	SLC4/35/13
CEP 147	STC4/40/70
657 CMT	63023
CRN 211	SB4/40/6
CRN 212	STC4/40/7
CRN 213	STC4/40/8
CRN 214	STC4/40/9
CRN 215	STC4/40/10
CRN 216	STC4/40/11
DRN 341	STC6/44/39
DRN 342	STC6/44/40
DRN 343	STC6/44/41
DRN 344	STC6/44/42
DRN 345	STC6/44/43
DRN 346	STC6/44/44
DRN 347	STC6/44/45
DRN 348	STC6/44/46
DRN 349	STC6/44/47
DRN 350	STC6/44/48
DRN 351	STC6/44/49
DRN 352	STC6/44/50
DRN 353	STC6/44/51
DRN 354	STC6/44/52
775 ERF	63012
ETY 174	STC4/40/69
EUJ 792	SB4/40/1
EX 8344	SLC4/35/62
GAY 50	STC4/40/3
GCT 181	STC6/44/80
GJR 965	63014
GNT 188	SLC4/35/5
GNT 190	STC4/40/4
GNT 587	STC4/40/20
GNT 961	STC4/40/14
GRP 105	STC4/40/72
GTH 576	STC6/44/98
GTK 992	63021
GUJ 457	STC4/40/31
GUJ 608	STC4/40/30
GUT 543	STC6/44/87
GUX 524	STC4/40/25
GUX 614	STC6/44/95
HAW 179	STC4/40/77
HAW 180	STC4/40/68
HAW 302	SLC4/35/54
HAW 303	SLC4/35/59
HAW 373	SLC4/35/22
HAW 374	SLC4/35/33
HAW 577	STC6/44/82
HAW 578	STC6/44/91
HAW 588	SLC4/35/57
HBW 505	4272
HCT 618	6308
HEA 433	SLC4/35/67
HED 480	STC4/40/85
HNT 49	SLC4/35/63
HNT 101	SLC4/35/23
HOD 57	SB4/40/2
704 HTB	6336
HUJ 619	STC6/44/81
JNT 763	STC6/44/100
JTL 469	63020
JUJ 264	STC4/40/18
JUX 270	STC4/40/17
JWF 176	STC4/40/27
JWW 316	STC4/40/15
KBX 630	63019
KDG 853	SLC4/35/26
KUJ 141	6306
KUX 412	6307
LDF 296	SLC6/41/101
LNY 307	SLC4/35/55
LOD 974	STC4/40/32
LWT 880	STC6/44/89
MKV 607	6302
MYR 500	SLC4/35/61
MYV 637	SLC6/42/113
NAB 756	63015
NAL 333	SLC4/35/64
NDE 555	STC4/40/79
NDE 620	STC4/40/38
NDE 689	SLC4/35/57
NDE 799	STC4/40/24
NHY 465	SLC4/35/53
NHY 637	SLC4/35/58
NLG 176	SLC4/35/29
NLR 850	SLC6/41/102
NNN 998	STC6/44/94
NT 4950	5102 *
NTB 955	SLC4/35/56
NVJ 664	63030
NWO 122	4271
ODE 40	STC4/40/71
ODE 182	STC6/44/90
ODE 280	STC6/44/92
OUP 578	STC6/44/100
OUP 579	STC6/44/73
OUP 580	STC4/40/84
OUP 581	STC4/40/17
OUP 582	STC4/40/83
OWU 771	63024
OWU 772	63025
OWU 773	63026
OWU 774	63027
OXT 23	6305
OXT 24	6309
PAE 596	SLC4/35/60
PHA 928	SLC4/35/28
PPT 212	SLC4/35/66
PPT 213	4273
PPT 214	4274
PPT 690	63011
PPT 850	63010
PXE 761	63013
RAT 645	63016
RHA 729	SLC4/35/65
RHW 233	6303
SDF 17	63017
SHT 468	6303
SUG 17	63016
SUG 19	6304
TAE 618	63018
UUB 931	63022
VRF 822	STC6/44/88
VTB 482	63028
YRF 732	STC6/44/93
YRF 733	STC6/44/97
YRF 734	STC6/44/99

Australia

Reg	Chassis
?????	SLC6/42/86
?????	SLC6/42/96
?????	6331
?????	6332
?????	6333
?????	6334

Brazil

Reg	Chassis
?????	SLC6/42/34

Ceylon

Reg	Chassis
IC 1467	SLC6/42/110
IC 2191	4301

Czechoslovakia

Reg	Chassis
O VIII 180	6147 *

India

Reg	Chassis
?????	6954 *

Portugal

Reg	Chassis
BL-18-52	SLC6/42/37
GC-18-68	SLC6/42/36

Singapore

Reg	Chassis
SH 190	STC4/40/??
SH 191	STC4/40/??
?????	STC4/40/??
?????	STC4/40/??

N.B. These four vehicles were STC4/40/74, 75, 76, & 78.

South Africa

Reg	Chassis
?????	6290 *
?????	6301

Uruguay

Reg	Chassis
?????	SLC6/42/35

A Sentinel Miscellany

The provision of a driver's-cab door on underfloor-engined vehicles was not unique to bodywork on Sentinels but was very much in the minority. In this unusual view through the cab of a vehicle from the Trimdon Motor Services fleet the open passenger door can be seen and a passenger directs a quizzical glance at the unknown photographer. *(John Banks Collection)*

The Commercial Motor Show in 1954. On the Burlingham stand was a service bus for Whieldon's Green Bus, Rugeley, built to the Blackpool coachbuilder's standard 44-seat front-entrance design. This vehicle (**775 ERF**) was one of six Sentinels which made such an impact on visitors at the 1954 Show. On page 27 it is shown as 775 ERF after delivery to Green Bus in February 1955. The vehicle later went to Camplejohn Brothers, Darfield, and was taken over with the Camplejohn business by Yorkshire Traction in 1961.

THE RIBBLE CONNECTION - The Ribble Sentinels were the largest group with any single operator; this, together with the dramatic "challenge-to-Leyland" circumstances surrounding their arrival in the North-West made them more than ordinarily interesting in a standard BET fleet. It is thus fitting that due attention be paid them, which we can do handsomely in a splendid series of images of both types when brand new. The first of them, a four-cylinder, 7ft 6ins-wide, 40-seat machine, fleet No. **2722** is seen on this page before it had been registered *(above)* and after registration as **CRN 211**. On the next two pages are views from several angles of No. **287** (**DRN 344**). *(All: Senior Transport Archive)*

141

142

As has been amply described in the pages of this book, Sentinels were few and far between, but there were enough for images of them to appear among the work of many amateur photographers of the 20th century. To round off the Ribble theme, No. **288** (**DRN 345**) was in a typical Carlisle streetscape *(above)* and No. **284** (**DRN 341**) was in Lowther Street, Carlisle *(below)*, on 17th August 1953. Both photographers went on to have important connections with Leyland Motors. Doug Jack was an official of the company as well as the author of the monumental "The Leyland Bus", and David Burnicle became Technical Director of Leyland Bus Ltd. *(A D Jack; David Burnicle)*

143

Above: The late Geoff Coxon's collection includes a few Sentinel images, taken in the mid-1960s, starting with **HAW 577** running for A.A. Motor Services, of Ayr.

Below: **KUJ 141**, the former demonstrator fitted with Duple Elizabethan coachwork, was photographed by Geoff Coxon in the livery of Carrs Coaches, New Silksworth, County Durham.

Above: Chapple, of Raglan, Monmouthshire, had **NWO 122** from April 1955. It was withdrawn from service in 1964 but remained in open storage at the depot, as shown in this picture, until sold for scrap in about 1967. The vehicle is now preserved. *(Geoff Coxon)*

Below: **CEP 147** was delivered to Mid-Wales Motorways, Newtown, in May 1951. After more than 18 years working for its original operator, it was destroyed by fire at Newtown garage on 19th July 1969, some two years after this photograph was taken. *(Geoff Coxon)*

Above: Another depot shot taken in Wales is of Rees & Williams **KBX 630**. Comment has already been made about the side beading on the Whitson bodywork - here it is seen from the nearside. The photograph dates from 1966, immediately before the vehicle was sold to Peters, of Pembrey. *(Geoff Coxon)*

Below: Sentinels from the lenses of the legendary Geoffrey Atkins are few but select. One that he could hardly avoid was the former Ribble vehicle on duty as a mobile café at Broad Marsh bus station in the photographer's home town of Nottingham. Geoffrey's infallible instinct caused him to place the vehicle in its setting with plenty of background, rather than taking it close up, thus making a picture in which the railway viaduct, the Barton Bedford/Plaxton coach (**870 HAL**) and office all play their part. *(G H F Atkins/© and Courtesy John Banks Collection)*

Above: Geoffrey Atkins concentrated on the East Midlands and, because Midland Red was one of his favourite fleets, was often to be found at St Margarets bus station in Leicester. On one such visit in search of Midland Red vehicles, he was tempted by this Boyer, of Rothley, Sentinel, nicely positioned and sunlit between platforms 3 and 4 awaiting its departure time for Loughborough. **HAW 578** had been a Sentinel experimental vehicle, also used as a demonstrator, which had a four-cylinder engine. It was sold to Boyer in 1953 and later passed to Midland Red as No. 4846.

Below: Midland Red **4847** (**GUT 543**) was another Sentinel acquired with the Boyer business. *(Both: G H F Atkins/© and Courtesy John Banks Collection)*

147

Above: As a native of the North-East, David Burnicle favoured his local operators and was thus on hand to record the influx of Sentinels into the Trimdon Motor Services fleet. This interesting picture, taken in West Hartlepool bus station on 30th July 1953, shows **JUX 270** in Sentinel livery working on hire to Trimdon. This was the undelivered European STC4/40 demonstrator, which Trimdon bought in December 1953 and reregistered OUP 581.

Below: **OUP 582** was delivered to Trimdon Motor Services in April 1954. In this 10th April 1954 view it was thus in its first days with the operator, and it had its original fleet number **26**, which was later changed to 22 (in December 1955). *(Both: David Burnicle)*

Trimdon Motor Services No. **9** (**PPT 213**) was one of three, Nos 5, 9 and 7 (PPT 212-4) SLC4s with Beadle 35-seat centre-entrance coach bodies, bought new in April 1954 as part of the job lot of Sentinels sold to Trimdon *(see page 24 for full details)*. It was photographed *(above)* in Oxford Road, West Hartlepool on 27th May 1954, believed working on hire to Richardson Brothers, whose garage was close by. The vehicle had the T M S transfer on the side, but was in the livery of the subsidiary Bluebird Coaches. In the picture below it has no T M S fleetname but carries the legend "Bluebird Coaches" in its nearside destination screen *(compare with PPT 212 on page 55)*. It was never legally owned by Bluebird *(see pages 68/9)*. (Above: David Burnicle; Below: John Banks Collection)

149

Upper: Brown, of Donnington Wood, Shropshire, was famous for its fleet of eight Sentinels. Three of these were photographed on 4th November 1966. **JUJ 264** was one of the two STC4 service buses. After completion in 1952 it was exhibited in Amsterdam where it disgraced itself by losing its engine. On return it was bought by Brown who used it until 1971. It is seen here at Oakengates on a local trip to Bell Gate.

Centre: Rear views are always scarce: early ones in colour even more so. **HNT 101**, originally a Sentinel demonstrator, was sold to Brown, Donnington Wood, in March 1953. Although preserved when withdrawn from service in late 1973, it was dismantled at Donnington Wood for use as spares.

Lower: The other STC4 was eight years old when acquired by Browns and gave them a further twelve before withdrawal in 1971. **GUJ 608** was bought for preservation by Richard Grey and now resides in the Aston Transport Museum. *(All: J D Howie)*

>> **Opposite page: GUJ 608** again, photographed in the Aston Transport Museum. Restored externally in the livery of its original operator (Maryland Coaches), the interior requires work to return it to original condition.

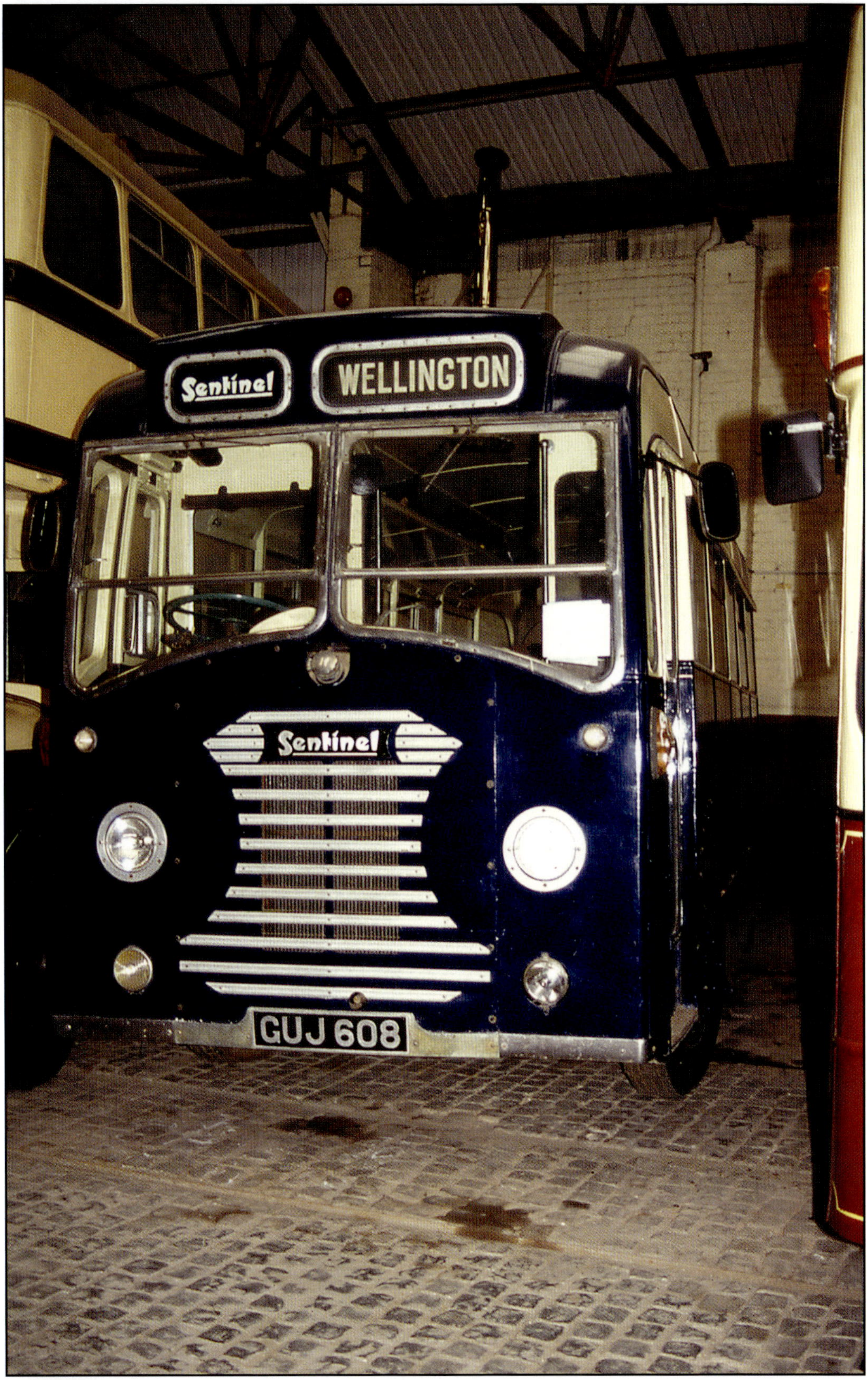
Sentinel
WELLINGTON
Sentinel
GUJ 608

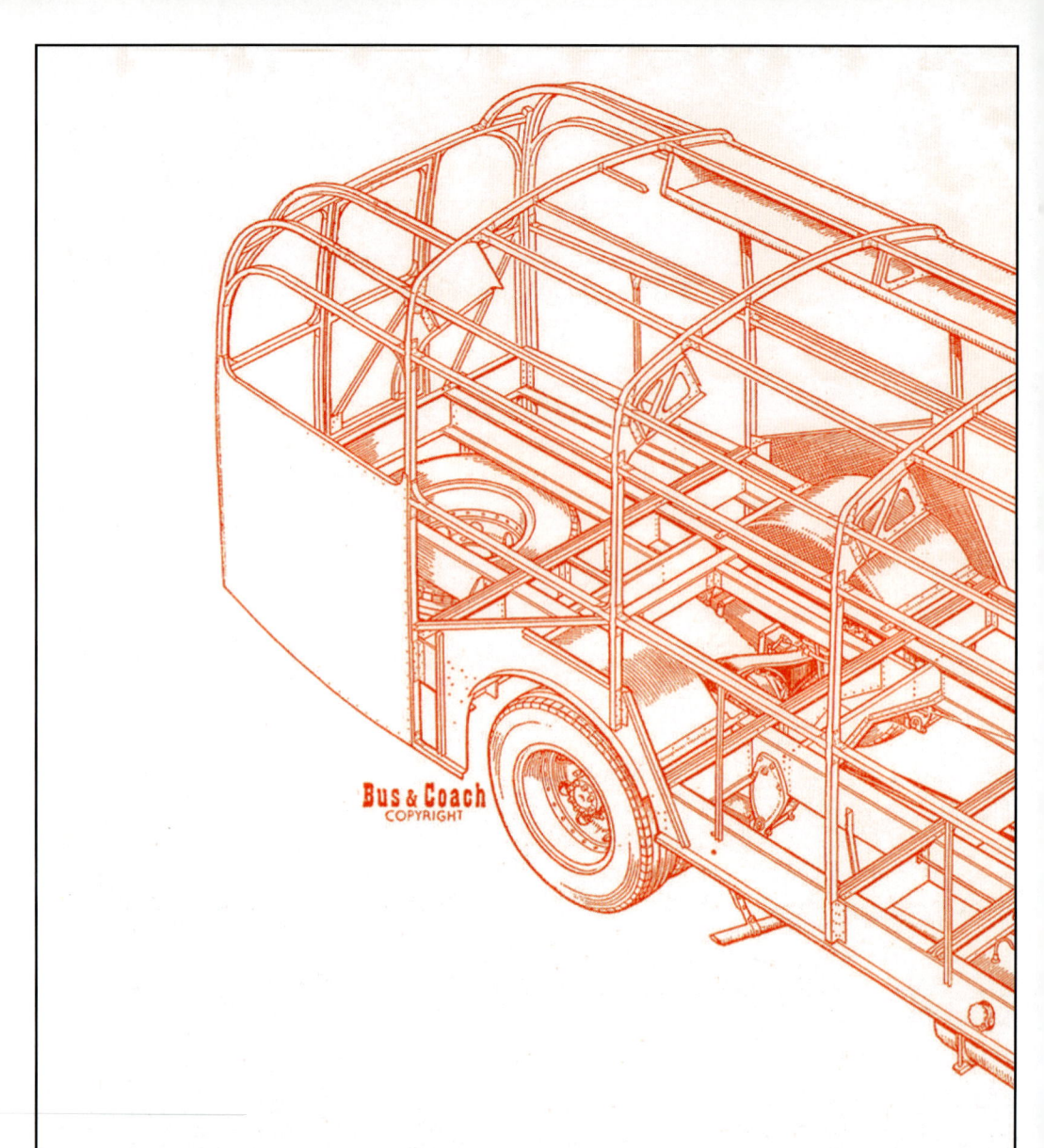

MAIN PARTICULARS

ENGINE : Sentinel-Ricardo, 4-cylinder 6-litre diesel.

TRANSMISSION : Single plate clutch, five-speed gear box, hypoid bevel final drive.

BRAKES : Girling with Lockheed hydraulic servo operation.

STEERING : Marles cam and roller.

SUSPENSION : Semi-elliptic, Girling Luvox dampers.

TYRES : 9.00—20in, twin rear.

WHEELBASE	14ft 9in
LENGTH OVERALL	27ft 6in
WIDTH OVERALL	7ft 6in
HEIGHT OVERALL	9ft 4in
FLOOR HEIGHT FROM GROUND (LADEN)	3ft 1in
OVERHANG (FRONT)	5ft 6in
OVERHANG (REAR)	7ft 3in
UNLADEN WEIGHT	5 tons 10 cwt 3 qrs
TURNING CIRCLE DIA.	62ft 9in

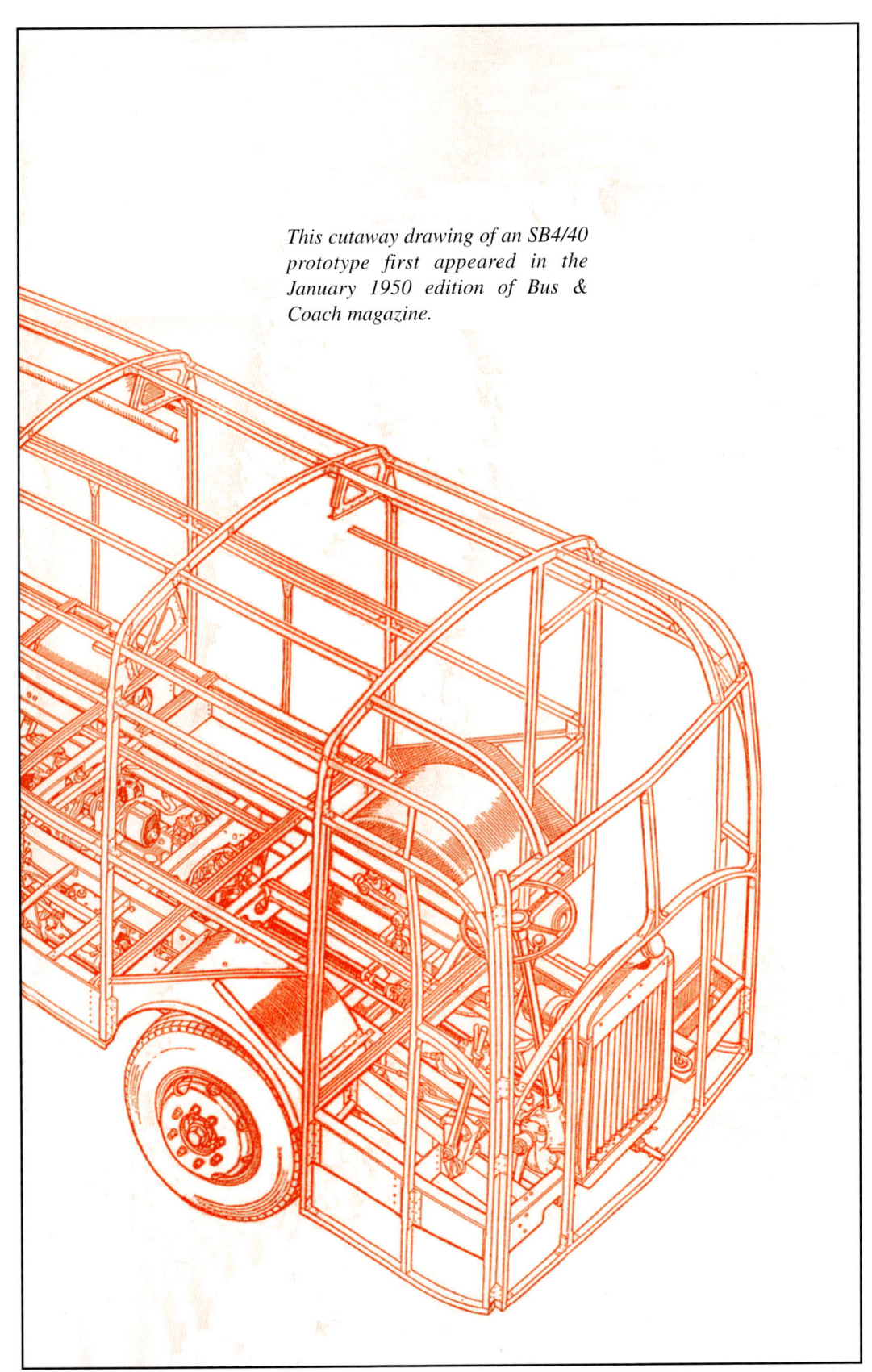

This cutaway drawing of an SB4/40 prototype first appeared in the January 1950 edition of Bus & Coach magazine.

BRITISH DESIGN FOR 1952

Bus & Coach

14 NOVEMBER 1951 · VOL. 23 NO. 276 · TWO SHILLINGS AND SIXPENCE

the operators' answer to the rising cost of fuel

The new Sentinel passenger 'bus

WITH COMFORTABLE SEATING FOR 44 PASSENGERS

.... "So you see Bill, with exceptionally low fuel consumption, on our routes it works out at something like 2½d. per Bus mile with a full load of 44 passengers, or 1/20th of a penny per passenger mile. Another thing, Bill, the engine is a 4-cylinder diesel job, horizontal underfloor type — so your driving position is ideal, plenty of forward control and all round vision. Yes, no doubt about it, this new Bus is the right answer."

Sentinel BUSES & COACHES

SENTINEL (SHREWSBURY) LIMITED Phone 2011 'Grams SENTNOLL

Passenger Transport

Vol. 103. No. 2627.

NOVEMBER 15TH, 1950

REGISTERED AT THE G.P.O. AS A NEWSPAPER.

30-Year Single

Sentinel Town and country buses...

BOYER LEICESTER

BOYER

GAY 50

SENTINEL (SHREWSBURY)
SHREWSBURY ENGL
TEL SHREWSBURY 2011 GRAMS SEN

JWW 316

May 13th, 1949   PASSENGER TRANSPORT   733

"Passenger Transport" Road Test No. 7

THE SENTINEL-BEADLE

Powered by a Sentinel underfloor oil engine, the new unit construction bus puts up good performances on a hilly west country route

FOR many years past, bus operators have shown a keen interest in various efforts of vehicle designers to evolve acceptable layouts for single-deckers capable of seating up to 40 passengers within the statutory limits of overall length governing types used in this country. As visitors to the Commercial Vehicle Exhibition in London will remember, the latest all-metal chassisless bus displayed by John C. Beadle (Coachbuilders) Ltd., of Dartford, Kent, attracted considerable attention by complying with that requirement. This old-established firm has achieved remarkable progress in developing chassisless bus designs during recent years and, as the following road test report reveals, its efforts have been attended by considerable success.

The model placed at the disposal of "Passenger Transport" for road testing, through the courtesy of Mr. B. V. Smith, M.I.Mech.E., M.Inst.T., Director and General Manager of the Western National Omnibus Co., Ltd., was a prototype bus which, at the time, was undergoing operational trials over one of the Company's routes in the Taunton area and the same route

The prototype Sentinel-Beadle chassisless single-decker operated by Western National Omnibus Co., Ltd., cornering on the ascent of Blagdon Hill.

156

was used as part of the trial run.

On arriving at Taunton, I was met by Mr. G. J. Brown, M.I.Mech.E., A.M.Inst.T., Chief Engineer of the Western National, accompanied by Mr. H. C. Scriven, Engineer-in-Charge of the Taunton area, and as the Beadle bus had been loaded to the equivalent weight of 40 passengers, no time was lost in preliminaries. We first proceeded to the nearby Taunton Depot, where the fuel tank was topped up on a level surface which also served for setting the Tapley performance and brake meters correctly to their zero readings; then, after checking the gross weight at 8 tons 4 cwt., we set off through the town on Route No. 208 to Churchinford over a very hilly route, in the direction of Honiton, that included the arduous ascent of Blagdon Hill which, over one mile in length, has a maximum gradient of 1 in 6 and several difficult corners.

As the report is confined to road performance, no more than brief reference can be made to details of Beadle chassisless construction. The basis of the design is a framework which, while providing the essential fixture points for the vehicle components, serves also as the underside of the body and supports the body framing, which, in turn, completes a structure of required strength and durability. Since the first prototype was produced in 1946, a number of Beadle chassisless buses, embodying different makes of chassis units, have been operated successfully by the Western and Southern National Companies, the latest example differing from previous types in that a Sentinel underfloor four-cylinder oil engine has been incorporated in the design. The new departure permits considerably increased body length for a given wheelbase, thus providing room for 40 comfortable seats.

PERFORMANCE AT A GLANCE

Make: Beadle all-metal chassisless 40-seater single-deck bus.

Date of Test: 9th March, 1949.

Gross Weight: (With load equivalent to 40 passengers) 8 tons 5 cwt.

Distance Covered: 42 miles.

Weather Conditions: Cold and dry.

Acceleration: 0 to 30 m.p.h. through gears: 25 seconds; 10 to 30 m.p.h. fourth gear only: 21 seconds (on 4th speed).

Tractive resistance at 20 m.p.h.: 35 lb. per ton.

Maximum gradient climbed: 1 in 6.

Maximum pull, climbing:
Fifth speed .... 50 lb. per ton.
Fourth speed .... 100 lb. per ton.
Third speed .... 200 lb. per ton.
Second speed .... 350 lb. per ton.
First speed .... (Not recorded).

Maximum road speed: 48 m.p.h.

Braking efficiency at 20 m.p.h.: hand brake, 28 per cent.; foot brake, 54 per cent.

Fuel consumption at 30 m.p.h. on hilly route: 11.93 m.p.g.

SPECIFICATION

Engine: Sentinel 4 cylinder diesel; bore 4⅞in., stroke 5½in.; displacement 6080 c.c.; maximum b.h.p. 90 at 2,000 r.p.m.; maximum torque 255 lb. ft.; maximum B.M.E.P. 103 lb. per sq. in.

Cooling System: Gilled tube radiator, shaft driven fan, water pump circulation.

Fuel System: 25-gallon tank; C.A.V. injection pump

Transmission:

Clutch: Borg & Beck 14in. diameter, single plate clutch.

Gearbox: Five speed David Brown gearbox with overdrive fifth speed.

Propeller Shaft: Two-piece Hardy-Spicer with spherically mounted intermediate bearing.

Rear Axle: Fully floating overhead worm, 4 bevel differential, ratio 6.75 to 1.

Tyres: 36in. x 8.00.

Road Springs: Reverse camber, semi-elliptic. Girling Luvax dampers.

Steering: High efficiency cam and roller, ratio 24.7 to 1.

Frame: No chassis. Beadle patented all-metal unit construction.

General Dimensions:
Overall length .... 27ft. 6in.
Overall width .... 7ft. 6in.
Wheelbase .... 14ft. 9in.
Track (front) .... 6ft. 4½in.
Track (rear) .... 5ft. 8in.
Body length .... 27ft. 4in.
Turning circle .... 65ft. 0in.
Unladen weight .... 5 tons 8 cwt.

An offside view of the Sentinel four-cylinder compression ignition engine which forms the power unit of the Beadle chassisless bus.

Producing a maximum output of 90 b.h.p. at 2,000 r.p.m., and the useful torque of 225 lb. ft. at half that speed, the Sentinel engine showed promise of good performance as the bus was being driven through Taunton traffic, and it was only at low crankshaft speeds that engine vibration could be detected. The route traversed during the first part of the test run provided everything one could desire for evaluating the qualities of Beadle construction from the passenger angle, and I was greatly impressed by the smooth motion, the absence of fore and aft pitch when uneven road surfaces were traversed, as well as perfect cornering stability. There is nothing even remotely resembling metallic resonance within the saloon which gives one the feeling of being driven over a rubberised road when, in fact, the surface is no better than it ought to be.

Though much nearer to the engine than in buses of conventional layout, passengers in the saloon have no oral evidence of the fact for, when pulling steadily, the power unit is commendably quiet. The first stretch of road clear from town traffic enabled me to make the usual test for tractive resistance and when coasting in neutral from a speed of 20 m.p.h., the figure of 35 lb. per ton was shown by the performance meter, proving that the 4,000 miles covered by the bus to date had eased off any "high spots" in the engine or transmission.

Numerous stiff gradients and sharp turns in the course that took us in the direction of the Blackdown Hills on the Somerset-Devon border prevented much use of fifth speed and on several of the hills I noticed that the meter was recording a steady pull of 100 lb. per ton when fourth speed was in action. The more exacting tests for maximum pull came a little later when Blagdon Hill was negotiated, and in accordance with my instructions, the driver delayed the changes into lower gears to produce accurate

A nearside frontal view of the same power unit showing the disposition of of the fuel pump and auxiliary drives.

results. Contrary to custom on this particular hill, the approach was made on fifth speed, but only for a sufficient time to ascertain the pull figure of 50 lb. per ton as shown by the meter. Ample engine torque through fourth speed enabled the bus to make good progress at a steady 20 m.p.h. for the next quarter of a mile and then, at the moment of changing into third, the fourth speed pull of 100 lb. per ton was again registered. A little later, second gear was needed to negotiate an acute left hand corner which produced the third gear pull of 200 lb. per ton, and now the gradient steepened to 1 in 6 as the Tapley meter dial swung round to show 350 lb. per ton after the driver had deliberately slowed down and re-accelerated for test purposes. The lowest ratio was not needed on Blagdon Hill, but on the strength of previous figures, I estimated the maximum first speed pull to be in the region of 480 lb. per ton, sufficient to enable the loaded bus to ascend a hill of about 1 in 4.6, given a reasonably good road surface.

Mindful of the need for quick acceleration for this type of bus, I took special care to obtain exact figures concerning vehicle performance, and found that the speed of 30 m.p.h. could be reached from a standing start with normal use of the gears in 25 seconds. This was accomplished in easy fashion by the Western National driver without disturbing the comfort of observers in the saloon or giving any indication that a critical acceleration test was in progress.

Then followed the alternative method of checking acceleration with the aid of Tapley meter readings, when, by causing the engine to run up to its maximum governed speed on each gear, the reading on the revolving dial was recorded at the highest point. Shown in lb. per ton these figures for each gear, on conversion into miles per hour per second, gave results as follows: Second speed 1.8; third 1.2; fourth 0.70; and fifth 0.45.

As will be gathered from the results, the ratios provided by the David Brown gear box are well suited to the torque characteristics of the Sentinel engine. These are: 0.75:1 for fifth speed; 1:1 fourth; 1.795:1 third; 3.24:1 second; 6.09:1 first, the final reduction in the rear axle being 6.75 to 1.

Another commendable feature demonstrated by the tests was the smooth transmission of engine power through the gears, propeller shaft and final drive, even under the very exacting conditions imposed by the final test for rolling acceleration from 10 to 30 m.p.h., when all the chassis units are pre-loaded and pre-stressed to a high degree at the start. The actual time occupied by the rolling acceleration test was 21 seconds in fourth speed.

Incidentally it may be mentioned that the Tapley tests provided further evidence of easy riding in the Beadle bus in that the movements of the revolving dial were unusually steady, by contrast with oscillations often occurring on such occasions.

Preliminary "cool drum" tests for braking efficiency at 20 m.p.h., gave a reading of 54 per cent. with 24.8 feet as the stopping distance for the Lockheed hydraulic brakes with vacuum servo assistance acting in large diameter drums. Hand brake action was less impressive as it only produced an efficiency of 28 per cent. and a stopping distance of 76 feet for reasons that became apparent later.

Having obtained all the necessary data concerning measured performance I tested out the driving position. Efforts to obtain maximum passenger accommodation have somewhat restricted the dimensions of the driving compartment and I found it a little difficult to insinuate my rather bulky person into the driving seat, the back of which is only 17 ins. from the rim of the steering wheel, but that was my fault for being too big.

Vision through the full fronted windscreen is good, the driver having a clear view of the nearside through the conveniently arranged front entrance. Clutch pedal, foot brake and accelerator and gear lever, are all in correct positions, but I was not altogether happy about the hand brake lever which does not give really full command of the operating linkage.

Like the rest of the bus, the driver's compartment is comfortable, quiet and free from draughts. Notwithstanding the unusual position of the power unit, Beadle designers have managed to overcome front suspension problems associated with this particular form of bus layout, and I was pleased to observe that the driver gets full benefit from the well proportioned and resilient springs which also absorb shocks that otherwise might reach the steering wheel.

Quick response of the engine to demands of rapid acceleration, enables the driver to get smartly away after picking up passengers, and to make good time on busy routes. The absence of engine noise in the driving compartment is a very agreeeble feature, although perhaps fresh drivers, accustomed to changing gear with the help of engine sounds, may have to look at the gear lever to find out which ratio is actually in use. It would be easy for a driver to remain in third speed for an unduly long time because the sound of the high engine revolutions would not warn him to engage fourth speed.

The five-speed gear box does its job quite smoothly in all speeds, quick and positive action of the clutch and selector mechanism encouraging the driver to make best use of third gear when occasion demands, instead of hanging too long on to fourth, thus imposing undue stresses upon the very willing engine.

To test the steering of the bus the vehicle was taken into the corners of a winding road at a fairly high speed to check the action of the steering with regard to easy control and castoring effect. In addition to perfect control as far as the steering mechanism itself is concerned, the bus is particularly light to handle by reason of the properly proportioned load distribution between the two axles, coupled with the qualities of suspension already mentioned. Besides cornering well, the Beadle bus holds the road nicely when travelling at its maximum speed of 48 m.p.h. with the engine running so smoothly that one almost forgets it is a diesel unit.

Before leaving the hilly country, one of the long descents was used for " warm drum " brake tests for which the foot brake was applied for a distance of about half a mile to induce conditions liable to impair retardation efficiency. Full application of the foot brake at 20 m.p.h. produced an efficiency of 54 per cent. as already recorded, a result denoting adequate frictional areas of shoes and drums, as well as good ventilation which allows rapid dissipation of heat.

Despite strenuous efforts on the hand brake it was not possible to improve on the original hand brake efficiency for, as already mentioned, it is difficult to get a good strong pull just when it is most needed.

The remainder of the 42 miles test trip was uneventful and served to confirm the generally good impression of this very useful type of bus which, from a constructional point of view, incorporates many desirable features too numerous to describe adequately in a road test report. On topping up the fuel tank at the Taunton depot on completing the trial run, the fuel consumption was calculated to be 11.93 m.p.g., a very satisfactory result considering the character of the route traversed and the fact that all the tests recorded above were included in the mileage over which the fuel consumption was measured.